I hope you enjoy
Katie's Story

# Katie's Story

## KARLA WEEKS

CROSSBOOKS

CrossBooks™
A Division of LifeWay
1663 Liberty Drive
Bloomington, IN 47403
www.crossbooks.com
Phone: 1-866-879-0502

© 2014 Karla Weeks. All rights reserved.

No part of this book may be reproduced, stored in a retrieval system, or transmitted by any means without the written permission of the author.

Scripture taken from the King James Version of the Bible.

Scriptures taken from the Holy Bible, New International Version®, NIV®. Copyright © 1973, 1978, 1984, 2011 by Biblica, Inc.™ Used by permission of Zondervan. All rights reserved worldwide. www.zondervan.com The "NIV" and "New International Version" are trademarks registered in the United States Patent and Trademark Office by Biblica, Inc.™ All rights reserved.

Scripture taken from the *Amplified Bible*, Copyright © 1954, 1958, 1962, 1964, 1965, 1987 by The Lockman Foundation. Used by permission.

First published by CrossBooks    06/09/2014

ISBN: 978-1-4627-3797-0 (sc)
ISBN: 978-1-4627-3798-7 (hc)
ISBN: 978-1-4627-3796-3 (e)

Library of Congress Control Number: 2014910047

Printed in the United States of America.

This book is printed on acid-free paper.

Any people depicted in stock imagery provided by Thinkstock are models, and such images are being used for illustrative purposes only.
Certain stock imagery © Thinkstock.

Because of the dynamic nature of the Internet, any web addresses or links contained in this book may have changed since publication and may no longer be valid. The views expressed in this work are solely those of the author and do not necessarily reflect the views of the publisher, and the publisher hereby disclaims any responsibility for them.

# *Dedication*

In loving dedication
to my single mother friends,
and, First Church of the Open Bible,
My children, Katrina and Randy,
To my husband, Russ.
And to single mother's
everywhere.
I love you All.

# Preface

The life of a single mother is one that presents many challenges. Do not get me wrong, married couples face challenges too. The big difference is that married couples can share responsibility. A large number of single mothers do not have the support of the father; therefore, they are in many ways alone.

I did not plan to be a single mother, it was not what I aspired to be when I grew up. Nonetheless, it happened. I divorced the father of my two children in 1987. During the time I ran a single parent household, I faced many of the same challenges other single mother's face. I learned to live on an almost nonexistent income and learned how to stretch that budget.

One of the biggest mistakes I think I made was constantly looking for the perfect love. I had the usual prerequisites including; he had to be good looking, he had to have a job, he had to be around my age, and regretfully, he had to make life fun. Unfortunately, I dragged my kids through each relationship. I did not just date the perfect love I married him too! A good friend told me once that I did not need to marry every man I dated. Wow! What a concept right. Well, she was right and after she told me that, I actually dated a few men and did not marry them.

From 1987 to 2000, I married, divorced, married, divorced, and married again. The last one stuck, we have been married for a whole 14 years! Why so many? I told you, I was looking for the perfect love. I can tell you that my husband is not perfect, (sorry babe), but I love that imperfect man and he loves the imperfect me. I can also tell you that I discovered something that I hope other single mothers can grasp. After many years of searching for that perfect love, I finally learned that the perfect love is Christ. Once you have that, your search for the perfect human love changes its face. You start looking for that Godly man.

I have been a member of the First Church of the Open Bible for about ten years. A few years after I started attending, I noticed the number of single mothers in the church. My heart broke for them. Having walked in their shoes, I knew they needed a support system. They also needed to know God more intimately. I talked to my pastor and asked if I could start a Single Mother's Support Group. The group lasted for a few years then eventually the mother's moved on and some married Godly men.

My desire to help single mother's never ended. I prayed continuously for God to show me what he wanted me to do to help single mothers. My answer came in the form of this book, Katie's Story. My desire is to serve my Savior, Jesus Christ, and show him to as many single mother's as I can find. I also feel strongly that parents and friends of a single mother could benefit from reading this story. As I mentioned before, single mothers have many challenges, and we do not always let people know what is really going on.

Katie's Story will let you walk in the shoes of a single mother who faces some of life's most challenging days. She experiences the pain from losing a loved one. She searches for the perfect love only to find heartache. She suffers through abuse and loneliness. Katie makes a mistake that creates separation from the people who love her most. Through Katie's life, we are reminded how God can use ordinary people to do extraordinary things for Him. Walk with Katie as she tells her story.

# Acknowledgement

I need to thank my parents Ralph and Karren for standing by me even when they did not understand why I continued to make the same mistakes. Their prayers helped me to see the light. For my children, Katrina and Randy, I dragged them down the path of my crazy life. Through it all, they continued to love and support me. Thank you to my husband, Russ, who has stood by my side through thick and through thin. In addition, to my best friend Sherry, who has been my prayer partner and encouraged me through many trials.

To my single mother friends who were willing to share their stories, their fears and their joyful times. (Incidentally, Katie's Story does not reflect any of the mothers' who attended group).

A special thank you to my Pastors, Bill and Kathy Hornback and the First Church of the Open Bible in Ottumwa, Iowa. The support I received for the Single Mother's Support Group was a Blessing. Thank you for your prayers and financial support for Katie's Story.

Most importantly, I thank my Savior, Jesus Christ, for taking on the sin of this world so that I can be forgiven. [1] John 3:16, For God so loved the world that he gave his only Son, that whosoever believeth in him should not perish, but have eternal life.

# Katie's Story
## Part One
# *Renewed Hope*

# Chapter One

Katie stood in the back of the room looking slowly and cautiously at each woman. She had attended these sessions for single mothers for several months, but never really told anyone her story. Heather, the leader of the Single Mother's Support Group walked toward her. Katie remembered the first time she attended the meeting. Heather welcomed her warmly and simply introduced her as Katie Stevens. Almost seven months later here she stood, nervous but ready to share her own story. Heather placed her hand on Katie's shoulder.

"Nervous?" she asked Katie.

"Yes," Katie replied, "I'm ready."

Katie walked slowly to the front of the room and sat in the front row. Heather stood in front of the room full of single mothers and opened the meeting in prayer. After a brief introduction, Katie took her place in the front of the group. This was not the usual format for the meetings. Typically, the group of women worked on bible studies and would have in-depth discussions concerning their lives, and discuss how they could allow God to lead them in their everyday activities. Today and the next few weeks, Katie would share her story. She cleared her throat and addressed the women.

"Thank you for coming," she began "I asked Heather if I could share my story. I hope that what I have gone through, what I have learned, can be a lesson and or an encouragement for you." She looked around the room again. Tears filled her eyes as she began telling her story. She started with the funeral of her parents.

"It was January 10, 1997, I was sixteen years old. Another winter snowstorm was beginning; large snowflakes began to float through the air. It was cold outside and cold inside my heart. My brother Todd and I sat in the back seat of the car." her mind went back to the events of that day.

Katie watched the scenery from the window of the car as they drove to the graveyard. Her eyes were swollen and stinging from hours of crying. She watched the snow as it floated down. She felt numb and lost as she watched out the window. Her mind was flooded with questions. How could this be? How could this have happened? Why my parents? Why did that truck run the red light? She thought about the words the preacher spoke. He talked about a loving God and heaven; but she wondered what kind of loving God would allow something like this to happen? How would she be able to go on without her parents?

Todd shifted his gaze from the window to his sister. They both looked at each other as the car came to a stop at the Cemetery. It was time for the graveside service. Todd stepped out of the car and walked around to help Katie out of the car. They both looked at the line of cars behind them. The snow mixed with ice was now coming down heavier and the wind had picked up sending the massive flakes swirling around and the ice stinging their faces as it hit them. After the graveside service, family and friends gathered at the church. Katie and Todd listened to the stories shared by those who attended. Many of the stories were about their parents when they were younger.

Katie brushed a tear from her cheek and looked again at the women who listened to her story. Breathing in deeply, "The next few months were busy," she continued.

Todd and Katie sat in the living room with their uncle Sonny. "Why don't you two move to Des Moines and live with us? We have plenty of room."

"Thanks Sonny, but I have a job and Katie still has to graduate," he looked at Katie "Unless you want to, I mean I am staying here but if you want to go, it might be better." he said.

"No, I want to stay!" was all she could say.

Todd explained that since Katie only had a year and a half left in school, and she was attending classes to become a nursing assistant, they should stay where they are. Reluctantly Sonny agreed.

"My brother was a real trooper," she told the women, "He moved back home giving up his apartment. Although our parents had life insurance, a good portion of the money went to pay off the house, the two family cars and the funeral. Todd worked for a local company as an electrical apprentice. And when money was tight, he took on odd jobs here and there." She smiled faintly then continued to explain the significant details of that day.

Katie went to her parent's room and sat on the bed. She thought about what Todd had told Sonny and wondered if she should go. "I don't want to leave this house," she whispered. She thought about the final moments at the hospital. When they arrived at the hospital, their mother was already gone and their father was just barely holding on. She remembered standing next to the bed as her father said his final good-bye. He told them both how much he loved them and how proud he was of them. He looked at Katie and told her she was a beautiful woman and she would make a great nurse someday. Then he looked at Todd and told him to take care of Katie.

Katie was relieved when it was time to take a break. She was emotional, telling her story was exhausting. She knew this would be hard for her, but also felt strongly that God wanted her to share her journey. She answered questions and talked to the women in the group as they snacked on finger foods during their break. Heather assured Katie that she was doing a fine job telling her story and she felt that the women would benefit from her life lessons. After the break, she told the women about Danny.

"Todd and Danny went to high school together." she smiled again then continued with her story. Danny did carpentry and roofing work for a local company after they graduated and Todd began working for the electric company. Katie always thought Danny was handsome. He was tall with wide shoulders, he had dark brown wavy hair and his green eyes sparkled mischievously. Danny spent a lot of time with them, helping to paint the house, repair the roof and other projects around the house. Todd was not upset when Danny and Katie started dating. He was surprised when Katie announced she was pregnant. Todd did not get upset, he simply pointed out that her education was important and she should finish high school.

Katie graduated high school in May 1998 and gave birth to a healthy baby boy the following December. She and Danny named him Robert Michael Marks-Stevens. Robert had blond hair like Katie and green eyes like Danny. She was so proud of her little boy. Danny was very attentive at first. His parents helped a lot with watching him while she worked. Although she had help, Katie knew what it was like to be a single mother. Danny did not live with them. He was there each night in the beginning and if he were not planning to be there, he would call.

As time passed, Robert was growing and Danny's visits were less frequent. Robert was playing in the sandbox in the back yard. He

*Katie's Story*

jumped up and started to run to his mother "look mom," he said as he carefully held out his hand to reveal his surprise, "a gran dad log leg."

"Nice, but maybe you can take it over to the fence and set it free," she told him.

As she watched Robert playing in the sand, she thought about Danny. She loved him but was tired of the separate lives they lived. After Robert was born, Todd had moved into his own apartment. Katie assumed Danny would move in or ask her to marry him and they would begin to share a life as a family. He did not. For the past year, he spent less and less time with the two of them and more time with his friends. Tonight was the night that she would put an end to their relationship, right after the birthday party.

Danny and Robert planned a party for Katie's twenty-first birthday. She did not feel much like celebrating but agreed to the festivities. Danny was going to arrive at six with pizza and cake. Katie was getting ready when Robert announced the arrival of Todd. She was surprised he was able to make it since he had been working out of town and did not think he would be off work.

"Danny asked me to watch Robert for a bit tonight so you two can go out." Todd told her.

"Todd, I don't think that's a good idea," she stated, "I told you I was breaking up with him."

"I know, and I understand, but perhaps, you should talk to him, try to work things out," he pleaded "I worry about Robert."

"I worry about Robert, too" she told him, "he loves his dad, but not having a real family is hard on us both…" She walked toward the bedroom to make sure Robert was still playing and not listening, "He helps us financially but he isn't here, he's out with his friends, we need him 365 days a year, twenty-four hours a day, not a day here and there."

Danny arrived thirty minutes late. He told them he was late because there were several people in the store. After they had their pizza and cake, it was time to open the presents. Todd presented his sister with tickets to see a play she had wanted to see. Robert ran to his room and came out with a box containing a lovely watch. He proudly announced that he helped pick it out. After the party, Katie told Danny she did not want to go out but did want him to stay a while, as she wanted to talk to him.

Once Todd left and Robert was in bed she knew she needed to talk to Danny. After a few minutes of small talk, she decided to tell him it was over. She told him that he could spend as much time as he wanted with Robert. The look in his eyes surprised and hurt her. She had never seen such a look of despair as she did at that moment. Danny sat silent for a few moments then without saying a word walked out the door.

"I remember standing there watching him pull out of the driveway, part of me wanted to run after him and the other part didn't." She looked toward the back of the room. She nodded to Heather and thanked the women for their time.

After the last person left, Katie and Heather walked toward their cars in the parking lot. Katie wanted to ask Heather about Tim but thought she should just leave well enough alone. After all, he did not owe her anything and was probably already married or dating someone by now. If only she had stopped running from God a long time ago, things could have been different now.

# Chapter Two

Katie walked through the park and thought of all the times she spent here with Robert when he was younger. She stopped to watch the children playing on the playground. The sound of the dog barking caught her attention and she turned to see what the ruckus was. A little terrier was chasing after a squirrel. She remembered when she and Robert had sat on a park bench and watched two squirrels chasing each other around and up a tree. "Funny squirrels," he said.

Memories of that day started to flood her mind. It was a typical fall day; she and Robert played in the leaves then sat on the bench for a snack. She remembered how tormented she was on that day. She was tired and had a headache from the lack of sleep. She was certain she was pregnant and she had just broken up with Danny. Now she would have to confront the truth and tell him that he was going to be a father again.

As she sat on the park bench, she thought about the events of that week. At that time, she worked as a nursing assistant at the Kendall House Care Center. She volunteered while she was in high school then started working after Robert was born. Three years later and she still had not gone back to school to be a nurse. Katie had wanted to be a nurse for as long as she could remember. She wondered if her parents would be disappointed with her life. Recently she transferred from second shift to first shift. This allowed her to spend the evenings with Robert and saved her some money in childcare. This would soon change she thought.

The shift change was how she first met Valerie, who would prove to be a good friend and her sister-in-law. At first, she did not know what to think of Valerie. She seemed like one of those religious types. Katie confided in Valerie that she might be pregnant. She told her about Danny and their relationship and about Robert. She also told her that she had recently broken up with Danny and why she thought she needed to. Valerie asked her if she loved him and she had to answer yes. She did love him she just wanted more. Valerie told her she would pray for her.

During her break at work, she called Danny and left a message for him to call her when he was off work. Later that night Danny returned her call and said he would stop by the next evening when he got off work. That night after Robert was in bed she paced the floor and cried as she had the past few nights. She was embarrassed and worried about what people would think when they learned she was going to have another child out of wedlock. Wedlock she thought to herself, having children, but not legally married. Plain and simple, people would think she was a loose woman.

Danny arrived just as he said he would. He spent some time playing with Robert and asked her about her new shift. She noticed that he was acting odd, but just thought he might have plans and wanted to leave. She asked him to have dinner with them and asked if he wanted to get Robert ready for bed and read him a story. She cleaned up the kitchen while Danny read to their son and wondered how she should start the conversation. She did not really want to just blurt out she was pregnant. She wondered if he would be upset, or think it was someone else's baby. She dismissed that thought; she knew Danny was aware that she did not date anyone except for him.

The sound of a honking horn brought Katie out of her trip down memory lane. She looked up to see Todd's car parked along the side of the road. Robert and Danie climbed out and ran to where she sat. Sometimes she thought about how hard it was to believe that Robert was already thirteen years old and Danie already eight. She mused how time seemed to slip away from her.

"Are you ok?" Robert asked Katie.

"Fine, just fine, I was just sitting here remembering all the times I brought you here to play as a child," she replied.

"Did you bring me, too?" Danie asked sheepishly.

"Actually, no, you were just a baby when we moved" she laughed. "I would bring Robert here at least once a week. We would pile the leaves and jump in them, then throw them in the air and let them float down on top of us."

She looked around the park again then stood and took Danie by the hand. "Time to go, we need to get something to eat and head to the church."

When Katie walked in the door of the support group room, she noticed there were more women than last week. She was not as nervous tonight as she was the first night. Heather met her at the back of the room.

"How are you holding up?" she questioned.

"Good, thanks" she said, and then pointed at the larger group "more women tonight I see."

"Yes, I guess the word got around, everyone wants to hear your story."

"Not sure if that's good or bad," she laughed.

They walked to the front and again Heather opened in prayer and introduced Katie to the group. She looked around the room and began to tell them about her day at the park. How just being at that park brought back memories. She told them about meeting Valerie. She also told them how she tried to prepare to break the news to Danny that he was going to be a father again.

"I know firsthand what it is like to go someplace and have to tell the doctor, neighbor, co-worker, or whomever, that, no, I am not married and yes these are my children!" She said. "People have a tendency to look at you like you're a loser or a bad person." She took a deep breath, "They don't have to tell us that, we tell ourselves that all the time." She looked around the room, and said "And just for the record, we are not losers, we are Gods children. We are Princesses of the King of Kings". She then continued her stroll down memory lane.

Robert was in bed and Danny came in and sat at the table. Katie finished putting the last dish in the cabinet and sat down across the table from him. They were both silent for a few moments. Then she finally told him she was pregnant. Her words jumbled as she told him about her doctor's appointment. She told him she had already spoken to Tina who enthusiastically agreed to baby-sit both of the kids. The entire time she talked to him, she did not look at him; she looked at her hands. When she finished she waited for a response. When none came, she looked up, shocked and a little mad at the expression on Danny's face.

Danny leaned back in his chair smiling "I figured you were pregnant."

"What?" she asked dumbly.

"Your color was off, you were grouchy and just didn't look like you felt good, just like when you were pregnant with Robert." Then he became serious.

"Oh." she murmured.

He looked her straight in the eyes and took her hands in his "I love you Katie, I love Robert, and I will love this little baby boy, too." Then he pulled a box out of his jacket pocket. He got down on one knee, "Will you marry me?"

Now crying and unable to form words, she shook her head yes and hugged him tightly.

"I know I should have done this a long time ago. I loved you before you were pregnant with Robert. I have known for a long time that I loved you and wanted to marry you, I'm sorry I didn't," he said.

She looked around the room and almost all the women had tears in their eyes. She laughed lightly then explained that he had the ring the night of her birthday party. The night she broke up with him, he was planning on proposing. "What a fool I was, I might have been saved a lot of heartache if I could relive that night."

She told the women how she told Valerie the news the next day and then told Todd. They set a wedding date for October 29. They did not have a large wedding. They both needed to work and decided that they would have a honeymoon after the baby was born and old enough to stay with his parents. Danny's parents and Todd were excited and all agreed that it took long enough for them to get married.

The day of the wedding, Valerie helped Katie get her hair done. She recalled standing in front of the mirror looking at the reflection looking back at her. She wore her mother's wedding dress. It was nothing fancy, just a long white dress with delicate lace around the neck and waist. She did not like wearing hats so she decided to have Valerie add some baby's breath to her hair. As she looked at her reflection, she realized how much she looked like her mother. Tears fell down her face as she wished that her parents could be there. Valerie held her hand and told her that they were probably watching and pleased that she was getting married to the love of her life. The wedding lasted a total of fifteen minutes. They went to the justice of peace. Danny's parents, Leslie and Dan, were there and Todd and Valerie. Robert was the ring bearer and they did not have a flower girl. After the wedding, they all went to Leslie and Dan's for cake.

Katie took a deep breath and wiped away the tears that fell down her face. "That was one of the happiest days of my life," she told them, "I loved Danny with all of my heart," She then suggested that this would be a good time to take a break. While the women gathered in groups to chat, Valerie and Katie walked out of the room into the hallway.

"Are you going to be ok?" Valerie asked her as she hugged her.

"Yes, it's hard, but I really think that this is what I am supposed to do." she answered.

"You are very brave and much loved."

They went back inside and Valerie asked Heather to come over and pray with them before Katie started talking again. Heather knew that this was hard for Katie and prayed that God would allow her to tell her story in hopes that the women hearing it would find it helpful and perhaps prevent them from making some of the same mistakes.

Katie cleared her throat and began to share more of her life story.

"Being married to Danny was different from just being the mother of his child," she laughed, "we never lived together before."

She told them how they were learning to put up with each other's habits. "Danny always left his wet towels on the floor and he would pester me about placing dishes in the sink with water in them to soak until I washed them," she giggled then her expression changed.

"It was December 8; we had been married six weeks. Danny was taking a shower and somehow slipped and fell as he was getting out.

We thought he was fine. He went to work and I did some things at the house before going to the store."

She just finished shopping and was about to pull out of the parking lot when her phone rang. It was Fred, Danny's boss.

"Katie, this is Fred," his voice sounded panicked.

"Is everything ok?" she asked.

"Katie, there's been an accident, you need to get to the hospital," he said.

"What happened?" she gasped.

"Danny fell off the roof, honey, it's not good, get here quickly," he said.

She quickly called Tina to see if she would meet her at the hospital and take Robert and the groceries home. Tina lived only a couple of blocks from the hospital and said she would meet her by the emergency room entrance. Katie told her she would explain when they got to the hospital. She did not want to say anything in front of Robert.

When she walked into the hospital, Fred was waiting for her. She looked around, but did not see Danny's parents. Fred was shaking and his color was pale. She asked where Danny was. Fred asked her to follow him and he led her down the hall to a small room. As they walked, he told her that Danny had a couple of dizzy spells that morning, but said it was nothing. Within a few minutes, the doctor walked in. The doctor explained that the injury Danny had suffered when he hit his head that morning probably caused him to have the dizzy spells. He probably had a concussion he explained. Danny fell from the second floor during a roofing job and hit his head on some lumber.

"Just like that, my husband was gone," she said through tears. "First my parents, then my husband." Her voice was shaky now and she held her hands tightly to try to control the shaking. "The day of the funeral was a lot like the day of my parent's funeral. It was snowing lightly that morning, then by the time we reached the gravesite the wind was blowing the snow." she paused for a moment. "Sure made the holidays that year a little less enjoyable." She smiled at Valerie and Todd, "Todd was a huge help, and he helped me keep it together for Robert's birthday and for Christmas. Todd was always there helping me."

She opened her bible and read [2]Psalm 18:2, 'The Lord is my rock, and my fortress, and my deliverer; my God, my strength, in whom I will trust; my buckler, and the horn of my salvation, and my high tower.' She closed her bible 'I didn't know this then, I wish I had. I had the chance, God was calling me, I just decided to run," looking at each woman slowly she said, "This is just a portion of my story or the book of my life as I have called it. I have many chapters of hard times. Times I ran from God, times of pain and heartaches. If you are running, please stop, allow God in your heart, allow him to be your rock, your fortress, your deliverer and strength, except his salvation and trust in him."

# Chapter Three

The single mothers support group was having a picnic with a guest speaker the next week so Katie was not planning on speaking. She did agree to go to the picnic with Valerie and Todd. Todd was in charge of grilling and Valerie was in charge of organizing the meal. Several of the women asked Katie questions about her struggles raising two children and asked questions about other parts of her life. A few of the women, including Valerie and Katie sat at one of the tables talking.

Valerie explained that she and Katie worked together at the nursing home. They talked a little while about childcare and how tired they would be when they got off work and how they had to "cowboy up" as they called it, and be a father and mother for their children at home. Valerie also told them how she could tell Katie did not know what to think whenever she would offer to pray with her over a problem.

"In fact," Valerie said, "Katie probably doesn't know about this, but," she smiled, "There was one night that I was asleep and woke up thinking about Katie. The feeling that I needed to pray for her was so overwhelming that I did, I climbed out of bed and started praying for her."

"I didn't know," Katie exclaimed, "not surprised, but, you never told me this."

"Well, I prayed for you for a long time, then a scripture came to my mind, it was one that I had read earlier in the day." She stopped and looked at the women, "I can't remember now exactly what it was. I know I opened my Bible and read that scripture and asked God to protect Katie and to give her strength."

Katie sat up straight in her seat and looked dumfounded for a moment," hold on, I know what scripture!" She reached into her bag and pulled out her tablet. "There was one night that I was really struggling. I did a lot of nights, but this one night I just felt as if my entire world was caving in on me. I sat on the foot of my bed and cried for hours. I paced the floor, I cried, I threw things. It was because I was so lonely. I was so lonely I really thought sometimes that I could just curl up and die. Then I went into the living room and on the table was that large family Bible you got for us as a wedding gift. I flipped it open and there was a scripture that seemed to just come out at me." She fiddled with the tablet a few seconds, "here it is, [3]Isaiah 41:10, this is from the Message Bible, Don't panic, I'm with you. There is no need to fear for I am your God, I will give you strength, and I will help you. I'll hold you steady; keep a firm grip on you."

Valerie looked at her then at the women. "That's the scripture," she said, "God was certainly with you and me that night."

Katie shook her head in agreement, "I remember that after I read that scripture I sat on the sofa and prayed. I asked God that if he was there and real, to give me the strength to go on. Then I went to bed and fell asleep."

Valerie continued her story, "The next morning I went to see Heather. I told her about Katie and how she needed prayer." Again, she looked at Katie and smiled, "Heather and I became intercessory

*Katie's Story*

prayer partners for you and she gave me advice on how to best help you."

Heather was listening and now jumped in with her part of the story "I knew Valerie was close to probably pushing you over the edge," she looked at each woman individually and continued. "Sometimes, us Christians are overly bold and pushy, hence the phrase "Bible Thumper." I explained to Valerie that what Katie needed at that time was a friend to listen, to offer her help when she could, to continue to pray for her, but not to try to push her or thump her."

One of the women asked, "So you told her not to talk about God?"

"No, not exactly, what I told her was to follow the leading of the Holy Spirit, and to remember that her personal relationship with God was her relationship. We did not know if Katie had a relationship with God or even knew anything about him and his loving grace. So at that point, we both just needed to be her friend and pray. God will lead us in the right direction."

The women continued to chat a few more minutes until Todd announced that the hot dogs and burgers were ready. They all filled their plates and found places to sit. Todd took a seat next to Valerie. He motioned to the table on the other side where Valerie's kids sat with Robert and Danie. He was thankful that the family was finally together. Heather sat down next to them and commented on the turnout for the event. "The speaker had an emergency and is unable to attend," she explained, "We will reschedule her later on."

"I was thinking, Katie, this was really a good idea to share your story," she paused and pointed to the crowd. "I think we should open our sessions up periodically for other women to share their personal stories, it would be good." Katie nodded in agreement.

"I think it helps when someone can open up and share with others in such a way, it shows that you're human, you make human mistakes, and like Katie said, maybe someone will learn from someone else's experiences. I was going to suggest we pray about this, but I believe this is something that God wants us to do, so I'll start working on getting this going," Heather concluded.

After everyone was finished eating, several decided to get a group together and play ball. Some decided to play Frisbee gulf and others were content to play on the playground equipment. Todd and Heather's husband, Mike, stayed at the shelter to visit.

"I bet you're glad to have your sister and the kids back home," Mike said.

"You bet! It was really hard when they were gone and we didn't know what was going on." Todd replied.

"Heather told me you took a lot on after your parents died, taking care of Katie and all."

"I made a promise to my father, but even if I hadn't promised I would still have done everything I could to help her."

"I probably would too," Mike told him, "And, if it wasn't for Katie working with Valerie, and Valerie knowing Heather, and both of them knowing Tim, you and Valerie wouldn't have met and married." he laughed.

"True, I wasn't really looking for anyone when Valerie and I met. I had stopped even looking." He shared with Mike how he had been dating his high school sweetheart Reba, when their parents died and later on, he was dating Tara when Danny died. Both, he pointed out, did not like him spending extra time helping Katie and broke up with him. He went on to say how when he first met Valerie he was instantly attracted and thankful that Tim had a project that needed to be done for the single mothers. "Otherwise, I may not have met Valerie or even allowed Jesus in my heart." Todd said. They continued to talk about sports and their jobs until it was time to leave.

# Chapter Four

Katie watched from the living room window as the five kids got on the school bus. Valerie had left for work a couple of hours before and Todd was feeding the horses and dogs. She was happy to be back in Iowa and thankful that she could stay with Todd and his family. While she lived in California, she went to college and was now a Registered Nurse. Shortly after graduation, she decided to move back to Iowa. She planned to stay with Todd until the Iowa Board of Nursing approved her license, she found a job and a place to live. Her license now approved, she began applying for open positions in the area. She hoped she would have her own place soon. Luckily, she had saved enough money to be able to keep her and the kids comfortable for a while.

Todd could see Katie looking out the window as he approached the house from the barn. He could tell she was in a daze and did not see him approaching. When he opened the door, she did not acknowledge he was there.

"You ok sis?" he questioned.

"Yes, yes I am fine, just thinking," she replied absently.

"You're worrying again about staying here, aren't you?"

"Sort of I guess," she admitted and poured them coffee.

"God will provide," he replied as he placed some banana nut bread on the table. "Valerie makes the best bread," he told her.

The two of them had some bread and coffee and made small talk for a few minutes. Todd was glad to have some time to visit with her without everyone else around. Having a full house has made it hard for them to have time to just sit and visit.

"Have you talked to Tim since you have been home?" Todd asked as he studied his sister's face.

She looked at him carefully before answering. "No, well yes, he stopped in the first night at the meeting." She thought about how her heart skipped a beat and fluttered when she watched him walk in the door.

"Really?" Todd's response brought her mind back to their conversation.

"We didn't talk, I looked up and he was there, then he was gone again."

"Hum," he replied "You could call him, I'm sure he would love to hear from you."

"Todd, I know you mean well, but I really don't think that's the best thing to do right now." She stopped and thought to herself how she would like to call him, but was afraid. She knew if she had stayed and not ran off with Franklin things may have turned out differently. She knew Tim liked her, but that was a long time ago.

"Well, I know it's hard for you, Tim and I are really good friends and he has asked about you often, he is glad you are home."

"He's been good to you and for that I am thankful," she said softly. "I know you two became good friends when you started working with him on the basement of the church."

"The single mother's father and daughter dance," he laughed. "Did I ever tell you what happened when I went to church that first time?"

"Tell me," she said anxious to hear his story.

Todd started telling her about the project that the two of them had worked on. Tim and Todd worked for the same company but not on the same crew. Tim knew Todd was looking for some work on the side and asked him to help with a project he had at the church. That was when he first met Pastor Grieg Nelson, who would later counsel him. He explained that at their first meeting the pastor was wearing jeans, a Harley coat and boots. He laughed and added that as it turned out he really was a biker and belonged to a Christian motor cycle group.

He told her how the days working with the men of the church were enjoyable. He really liked them and was surprised that they seemed to be just normal people. He had always thought of Christian men as being weak.

"We talked about you," Todd said to Katie as she listened intently to his account.

"What?" she asked surprised.

"Yea, I was worried about you, after Danny. I was concerned about how you would handle being a single mother." He looked directly into her eyes, "I asked for advice for how to help you and we discussed inviting you to attend one of the single mother sessions, instead, I asked you to the dance."

He told her about Valerie and Heather coming in to do some work and how he kept sneaking glances at Valerie. He did not want to talk to her because he did not want to get involved with anyone at that time. He pointed out that his past two relationships had not worked out well for him. When Katie apologized, he quickly told her not to, Valerie was his life match, and the other two were not. He remembered thinking that she was the prettiest redhead he had ever laid eyes on.

Tim had invited Todd to church one Sunday morning. Although he hesitated, he decided to go. He told her how he got there late so he could sit in the back and just watch and be able to leave without anyone seeing him. That did not work, when the congregation began shaking hands and greeting everyone, Tim spotted him.

The music was what first started getting to him. He recalled how the words in the songs that they sang really touched his heart. "It was as if each song was personally selected just for me," he recalled. The sermon that day was about [4]David, how God called him a man after his own heart. David complained about God not being there.

"Grieg, the minister, was actually awesome. He threw his arms in the air and in and a loud voice says,[5] Lord, why are you standing aloof and far away? Why do you hide when I need you the most? Then he walked across the stage and continued even louder, why do you ignore my cries for help, why have you abandoned me?" He stopped a moment and smiled, "My heart is beating as hard and fast now as it did that day." He became serious again, "That's exactly what I thought. In all the chaos in my life and your life, I often wanted to know, where was God, what was he doing to help?" Todd told Katie how he was shifting uncomfortably in his seat and wondered if people were looking at him.

"Then the pastor said, we all go through things we do not understand, we are hurt, dragged down and emotionally drained. He said we are not alone that [6]God promised he would always be there," he stopped and nodded his head. "He said we have problems, but, God is there in the midst. He is walking by our side and sometimes even carrying us. He said that we can talk to God, he hears us, and if we would allow God, he would help us." He smiled and shook his head, "then, I got up and left."

"What? You left," baffled by what he had just said, "I thought..."

"I did, but not until later," he interrupted her. He told her how he spent the next several hours pacing and very confused. Tim called and came over that night and they talked for a long time. "That was when I asked Christ to come into my heart."

"Wow, I had no idea," she said.

"It was Tim who suggested that I talk to pastor Nelson, so I did counseling with him for several weeks."

For a few minutes, she sat there thinking about his experience. She knew it was hard for him to understand how much God loved him because it was hard for her to believe that God loved her.

"I'm thankful that Tim was there for you."

# Chapter Five

Katie was excited to receive a call from one of the doctor's office she had applied to work. She was scheduled for an interview the following Monday. She could hardly wait for Todd and Valerie to get home so she could share the news. Once she had a job she could start looking for a place for her and the kids. She heard a car door and hurried to the door thinking it was Todd or Valerie.

"Hi, Tim," she said surprised.

"Hi," he said nervously.

"Todd isn't home yet, but come on in, he'll be here soon," she offered.

Tim placed his jacket on the chair and sat down. He looked at Katie and wondered if he had the nerve to ask her. He fiddled a bit with the pillow and looked around the room. "They sure have a nice place don't they?" he said.

"Yes they do, it's a bit crowded right now, but hopefully that will soon change," she said and then she told him about her interview.

"I actually came to see you," he blurted out.

Katie sat down in a chair opposite his chair and held her shaking hands in her lap.

"I wondered if maybe, well it's been a long time since I have seen you and," he stopped and looked at her hoping that he could find the words he was looking for, "Would you like to go out to dinner or something?"

Katie smiled and told him she would be happy to. They arranged to go out after the single mother's session that night. She shared with him that tonight's meeting would be another emotionally draining session as she intended on talking about Todd's accident and the days that followed. Tim asked if she cared if he came in and listened while she talked.

"Please do, I need all the support I can get!" she said.

Todd and Valerie arrived shortly after and she shared her good news about the interview and the date for pizza after that night's meeting. She told the kids they would soon be able to look for their own place. The kids were excited and Valerie teased that they probably just wanted their rooms back.

All the women had gathered in the room. Heather pointed out that if the group kept growing they would need to move to a larger room. Heather, Valerie and Katie prayed together before the introductions and Katie began again with her testimony.

"As you have heard so far, I have had much heartache in my life. It seemed to me that my life was just a series of tragic events." She looked toward the back of the room at Todd then Tim. "Well, unfortunately, there was more to come." She explained to the women that unbeknownst to her, Todd had planned to ask Valerie to marry him, but things quickly changed.

Todd and his crew were working at a construction site where they were adding on to an existing building. Todd's crew would be working inside one section and the other contractors were working outside. There was a problem so Todd and one of the co-workers needed to go to the other contractor's site to talk to their supervisor. On their way over, they stopped to watch the crane operator lifting a large bundle of steel. They thought they were at a safe distance. Todd waved at the foreman and motioned for Roy to follow him.

As Todd started to walk toward the foreman, he heard a loud clanging sound. He looked up toward the bundle of steal and again heard clanging. He turned toward Roy and started to run yelling for him to run also. Roy heard a swishing sound and looked over his shoulder in time to see Todd diving over some pipes. Clanging, crashing sounds and dust filled the air as the steel started crashing to the ground. Roy was the first one to reach Todd. Todd's leg was pinned under a pile of steel. His own crew could hear Todd screaming and they rushed to see what had happened. One of the men ran to Tim to let him know what happened. Roy ensured someone called for help. The safety manager and foreman had started barking out orders for the men to clear a path for the ambulance and for someone to wait for them to arrive at the gate and direct them in.

Tim arrived and knelt down next to Todd. By this time, Todd was in and out of consciousness. Tim fell to his knees and began fervently praying for his friend's life. He prayed for strength and wisdom for the medical professionals, and then he prayed for Katie, Robert and Valerie. When he was finished he looked around, he expected to see the others looking at him, thinking he was crazy, but instead most of the men were also on their knees and the ones who were not had stopped and their heads were bowed.

"Roy told me later that everyone really respected Tim and Todd. It is amazing how we respond during times of pain. We panic or we pray, Tim prayed, as far as I know he never wavered, he never panicked."

"It was hard not knowing what was going to happen," she told them. "He was taken to Iowa City Hospital. I rode with Valerie and Tim and the pastor and his wife followed behind us." She told them how the car ride seemed to last forever. When they arrived, no one knew what to expect. They waited for what seemed like an eternity for the doctor to come out and see them. He explained that the injury was serious and they may not be able to save the leg. The doctor told them that Todd was getting ready for surgery.

"Keep in mind at this time I was not a Christian. I was actually mad at God. I blamed him for Todd's accident, just like I blamed him for my parents and for Danny's death." She wiped away her tears. "As you know, Todd did lose his leg." The women in the room were crying and Heather suggests a small break. Katie was glad to have a few moments to pull her thoughts together.

Tim went to Katie and put his arms around her. She felt comfortable in his embrace. She wiped her eyes and looked up at him "Thank you, thank you for being there for my brother during everything that happened to him, thank you for everything you have done that I never appreciated before," she said through broken sobs.

She took her place back at the front and began again. "There were a lot of changes that had to be made. We moved Todd out of his little apartment and into a house that was on one level." She told how they were lucky that Roy happened to have a place open up just at the time they needed it. She also told them how in the middle of all of this Valerie had a baby shower for her.

"Todd wanted to be there when Danie Marie was born, but unfortunately Danie had plans of her own," she laughed. "So the day they were moving Todd's belongings, I was having a baby. She was two weeks old before Todd finally got to hold her." She grew serious again and told them how she had started pulling away from

Todd at that time. She inserted that his newfound faith was a source of aggravation for her. He did not stop talking about how God would see him through this trial and how he trusted that all things would work out. "I started pulling back from Todd; I didn't understand him or his God."

She continued to tell the women about the day that Todd told her he asked Valerie to marry him. Tim had helped Todd to get everything together for a nice candlelight dinner at the church. Todd wanted to ask for her hand in the place that he first fell in love with her. Katie was not happy about the engagement. She tried to hide her anger but Todd had noticed it.

"Are you mad?" he asked her.

"No, just upset that you didn't even tell me you were planning on asking her."

"Don't you like Valerie?"

"Yes, but it's so soon, you are just now getting to where you can walk and now you're going to marry someone with three kids!" she shot at him angrily.

During the next month, Valerie tried to call Katie, but she did not answer the phone and did not return her calls. Valerie was worried about her. Katie was on the schedule to be back to work two weeks ago, but instead she quit her job. Valerie learned she was working for another nursing home in town. Finally, she decided to just stop by and try to catch her at home. When she pulled in the driveway of Katie's house, she asked God to help her.

Valerie told Katie that they had set the wedding date for January 12. She watched for a reaction and when she did not respond, she pressed her further.

"I know you think this is sudden, and that you're probably worried about Todd stepping into a ready-made family. But Katie, I love your brother." She could see tears welling up in Katie's eyes. "We want you to be happy for us and to trust us."

Katie stood and moved toward Valerie and hugged her tightly. "I'm sorry, I am happy, just worried," she said between sobs. "And, I guess I am a little jealous."

"I want you to stand up with me, be my maid-of-honor."

"Of course I will."

The following months kept them busy with wedding preparations. Katie had many ideas for the wedding. She always dreamed of the perfect wedding. Although Todd said money was not a problem for the wedding, the girls decided to save money and make many of the decorations themselves. Katie's house was loaded with tulle, flowers, and a large variety of crafts.

"You are really good at this, you should be a wedding planner." Valerie told her one day after Katie showed her the plans for the dining area.

"I don't think I'm that good, but I really do enjoy this." She stopped and looked at the vase that had just arrived. She held it up and read the poem on the side as tears rolled down her face.

"What's wrong?" Valerie asked.

"Todd's getting married and mom and dad will not be here to celebrate." She held up the vase to show her. "I found this in a magazine and thought we should place some flowers with a card attached on the table next to the vase. Then people entering can write down the name of the person who is not able to be there but close to our hearts," she wiped the tears away, "Like, mom and dad and Danny."

Katie looked out at the women and again noticed how they were crying. "Guess we should remember not to wear make-up for this single mothers group," she laughed as she wiped away tears. The women laughed and chatted for a few minutes as Katie gathered her thoughts.

"Well, during the time we were planning the wedding was when I started dating Franklin." She took in a deep breath, "however, that is a story for the next session." She thanked everyone and turned it over to Heather.

# Chapter Six

Valerie and Katie sat at the table having coffee and making plans for the day. Since Valerie was off work, they thought they would get some shopping done and maybe even catch a movie.

"So, did you and Tim have a nice dinner last night?" Valerie questioned as she winked at Katie.

"It was really nice," she said deliberately not giving her any additional information.

"So, where did you go?"

"Pizza house," she replied with a smile. "We should go to that new store in the mall this afternoon." Again, she deliberately teased Valerie.

Valerie did not reply she just stared at Katie. After a few minutes, Katie finally told her that they talked about the kids and her plans now that she was back at home. Disappointed, Valerie insisted that he was nervous and that she was sure he really liked her. Katie knew that she was right and finally told her that they were going out on Saturday evening.

The next day Katie went to her interview and felt very confident she would receive a call. Later that day she did get a call from the human resources department and they offered her the job. She was so excited; she sent a text message to Tim to let him know. She had to go through the initial orientation on Monday. Of all the places she applied for a job, she really wanted to work at the clinic. She would work Monday thru Friday and have weekends and holidays off. It was full time and offered benefits and a retirement package. It also had a handsome wage that for her meant that she would be able to begin looking for a place to live.

After three hours of shopping, they decided to grab a bite for lunch before heading to the movies.

"We should do this again!" Valerie told her "But, next time I think I will wear comfortable shoes!"

Katie laughed, "I agree, on both counts!"

"I think Danie will like the dress you got her," Valerie said as she picked up her vibrating phone.

Katie ordered their lunch as Valerie talked to Todd. She was glad to spend some time with Valerie.

"Apple got hurt today." She explained to Katie that her horse was spooked and ran off, running right into some bobbed-wire fence. She would need to help Todd because Apple sometimes would not cooperate with him. They asked the waiter to make their order to go.

She was home alone in a quiet house. Everyone was gone at least until about 3:30 so she planned to catch up on some reading and go over the notes for her next session with the women. She made some hot tea and curled up on the sofa with her book. She began to read about getting out of a [7]pit. As she read, her mind drifted off to her past.

She had been so angry for so long. It really did start for her when her parents passed away. She never really grieved; she looked for comfort and found it with Danny. She thought about how she rebounded. When you think of a rebound, you think solely on a person jumping into another relationship when one has just ended abruptly. For her, it was a relationship, but one with her parents. She thought about how it was the same as losing a boyfriend. Her parents were her world, her safety net. With her parents gone, she clung to Danny.

That was where my pit began she told herself as she read some more. She thought about Danny, how after his death she slid deeper into her pit of self-pity and hurt. Then Todd's accident added more mud that just kept the sides of the pit slippery. She took a few minutes to thank God for pulling her out of that pit. She thought about other women and even men who found themselves in situations that caused so much pain that they slipped away from God. She said a silent prayer for people who needed God's help.

Quickly she grabbed her paper and pen and jotted down a few notes that she wanted to share with the women at the next session. As she was going over her notes the phone rang, it was Heather. They discussed the next session and discussed trying to wrap things up in the next two meetings. The women's group would be having their annual retreat so they needed to start getting organized.

She started reviewing her notes again and made some changes. She knew she wanted to tell them about Franklin and definitely tell them about how God had changed her life. As she recalled the time she spent with Franklin, she began to feel guilty again for what her children had to endure. She thought about her past, and how she made bad decisions, and how her children suffered from the decisions she made. She never wanted to hurt them. Tears fell down her cheeks as she remembered the first time things had gone bad.

Franklin was the jealous type and daily it seemed to get worse. Katie was in the yard with Robert and Danie when one of the winery employees came over to say hi. He played with Robert for a few minutes and talked about his own children. Franklin came over, demanded that he get back to work and ordered Katie to take the kids in the house. Robert was playing with his cars and asked why he had to go inside. Franklin snapped, he yanked Robert up by the arm and told him never to talk back or to question him again. Katie was scared; she took the kids to the house and did not say a word to Franklin. She tried to calm Robert down with some cookies and milk. Later that night she and Franklin had their first fight.

As she sat there remembering that day, she told herself that she would never allow anyone to treat her children or her in that manner again. That day was the beginning of several bad days. She feared for her children and the baggage they may be carrying. She talked to them often about their feelings and even sent them to counselors. She prayed that they would trust in God and allow him to carry their burdens and heal their hearts.

Tim called and they talked for a long time. He could sense that something was bothering her and he questioned her. She began to tell him about some of the things she and the children had gone through. He told her that she had done the right thing by getting the children in Christian counseling. He believed that they would be fine. He shared some of his own struggles with Jacob. He told her he made mistakes and often had to ask both Jacob and God for forgiveness. "Nothing like daily seeking God's grace," he told her. He told her to continue to trust in God and raise her children in the way that they should go.

Katie told him how she would become overly stressed and angry. She would take her anger out on her kids, snapping at them over little things. She told him how she hoped they would forgive her.

"Thank you for listening to me," She said.

Katie was thankful for Tim's advice. She wished again that she had not run away all those years ago. She wondered if Tim would ever be able to fully forgive and trust her again. She hoped he would.

# Chapter Seven

"Tonight, I want to tell you about Franklin," she began. She noticed she was trembling and tried to calm down. "Funny, I left him in December of 2005 and I still get a feeling of fear when I think about him or talk about him." She fumbled with her notes. "I heard once that the Bible says 365 times do not be afraid or do not fear. I have never counted how many times, but, I think that 365 days a year I can trust and not be afraid." She breathed in deeply and said a silent prayer for strength. "I guess the best place to start is when Franklin and I first met."

Katie was busy making more wedding decorations, this time for the dining tables. She fussed over every little detail as if it were her own wedding. Occasionally she would get a twinge of jealousy. She wished she were in love, planning her own wedding and had a full family. She wondered about her date tonight if he would be the one. Tonight she had a blind date. Her friend Rhonda's boyfriend had a single friend so she thought she would try to play matchmaker. Part of her wanted to call and cancel the date, but the lonely part of her overruled.

Katie looked around the crowded room until she spotted Rhonda. She made her way through the crowd thinking how much it smelled.

Heavy smoke filled the room and she could detect the smell of beer mixed with something she could not identify. She had never been in a bar before and suddenly realized she did not like it. Other than an occasional glass of wine, she never drank. As she looked around at the people in the bar she realized many of them were drunk or on their way there. For a moment, she thought she should turn around and leave before Rhonda spotted her.

"Katie," yelled Rhonda over the noisy bar, "sit here," she motioned.

Katie sat next to her and placed her hands in her lap hoping no one noticed she was shaky and uneasy about being there.

"Katie, this is Leo my boyfriend and this is Franklin." She slurred her words, which confirmed she too had a lot to drink.

Everyone said hello and started to make small talk. Katie strained to hear them and again regretted having had come in the first place. Franklin was her blind date. He was not overly handsome and had a bump on his long nose that made her wonder if it had been broken. Perhaps in a bar fight she told herself. Franklin nodded toward the waitress who had asked if she wanted something to drink. Before she could ask for a diet soda, Rhonda ordered her what she thought she called a Jell-O shot. She did not want to embarrass herself in front of the others so she smiled and agreed on the drink selection.

The four of them talked and joked throughout the night. Every time Katie finished a Jell-O shot, it seemed there was another one there to take its place. She felt different and found herself laughing at things she would not normally laugh at. She glanced above the bar and noticed it was 11:00. Tina was watching the kids and she told her she would be home at 11:30. She knew she was drunk and was not going to be able to drive. She did not want to call her brother or Valerie to pick her up and she knew she did not want Rhonda or the men to take her home in their condition. She told them she needed to leave and headed out the door before anyone could object.

The next morning she opened her eyes slowly and sat up. She looked around her room then placed her head in her hands. Her head was throbbing and she smelled like a bar. "How'd I get home?" she asked herself. She bolted straight off the bed. "Tim," she said horrified. She was walking home and Tim stopped to pick her up. She gasped, "He said he was staying to tend to the kids." Her heart raced and she began to panic. Tim had stayed to watch her children because she was drunk. She hesitated before opening up the door and facing him.

Tim was sitting at the table with Robert and Jacob and was feeding Danie from a bottle. He looked up when she walked into the room, but did not smile. He nodded to the counter, "There's coffee and aspirin," he said.

She knew Tim was upset with her. He usually smiled when she walked into the room, but not this morning. He looked disappointed and hurt. Robert began telling her how Tim got their breakfast and even changed his sister's diaper. At that, both boys began to laugh loudly and hold their noses. She was too embarrassed to look at Tim. She walked over, took Danie, and sat where she did not have to look him in the face. She cooed and cuddled with Danie and asked Robert about his night with Tina.

After the boys left for the bedroom, Tim started to clear the table.

"I'll get that, you've done enough," Katie said.

Tim looked at her for a long moment. He was about to say something then changed his mind and moved toward the kitchen sink with the dishes.

"I've never done anything like this before," she started to explain.

He slowly turned around "Tina was worried, she was about to call Todd when we got here," his voice was shaky and she could tell he was holding back his anger.

"I should have called her," she ruffled up a bit, "I didn't want to drive and didn't want to have my friends drive me so I thought I would walk. And besides, how did you know where I was to pick me up?"

"You shouldn't have needed to call, you shouldn't have gone out and got drunk," he scolded. "I was heading back from the movies and I saw you walking."

"Who do you think you are?" she hissed angrily, trying to keep her voice low so the boys did not hear her. "You are not my father, brother or boyfriend!"

Without another word, Tim got Jacob and left. She spent the rest of the day wondering if he would call Todd or Valerie and tell on her. She felt like a school kid who was afraid her parents would find out she did something wrong. She did not feel good and her head still hurt. She called Tina to apologize and told her it would not happen again. Later when Valerie called, she did not let on like she or Todd knew anything. They did not even know she had a blind date.

Franklin called and thanked her for joining them and told her how much fun he had. He hoped she was not late getting home to her children and said he should have taken her or not let her drink so much. He asked if he could see her again, but this time not in a loud bar or drinking. They made plans for dinner and a movie for the following weekend. She was sure to tell him she needed to secure childcare first and would call him in a day or so and confirm.

Katie and Valerie were putting some final touches on the wedding plans and making decorations. Flower arrangements had been made using Christmas Holly. Mistletoe was prepared and ready to hang throughout the church. She was relieved that no one had mentioned her night out so she was sure Tim had not spilled the beans. She told Valerie about Franklin and asked if she could watch the kids so they could go out. Valerie asked several questions in which she was unable to answer. The only thing she really knew or remembered was what he looked like and that he said he was a mechanic. Valerie said she would be happy to watch the kids and wanted a full report.

Franklin ordered their pizza and drinks and they talked and laughed about the movie. She was having a good time. She learned he was originally from Vegas and moved here a couple of years ago with a girlfriend. Their relationship ended, but he did not seem to want to discuss it. He talked about his family and that they owned a winery. He said he planned to go home after the first of the year for a visit. He worked with Leo and they became friends right away. After their pizza was finished, he offered to take her to pick up the children, but she insisted it was not a good time. He drove her home and waited for her to get in her car and leave before leaving himself.

As she drove, she wondered about his ex-girlfriend and wondered why they broke up. She thought it was best not to pry in his business. She had a good time and decided that she would like to see him again if he asked her. She was distracted with her thoughts and did not notice that he had followed her. He parked the car a few houses down and watched her enter the home. He looked at his watch and waited for her to leave.

"I didn't know he was waiting and watching until later. He had jealous rages and in one of the rages he accused me of having a fling with Tim and mentioned his watching and waiting for me that night. Looking at the women she shook her head, "I think if I had known he did this before we went to Vegas, I would not have continued dating him. The first of many mistakes I would make."

The wedding was beautiful and the newlyweds were on a two week honeymoon in Florida. Between Katie, Valerie's parents and Ken, Valerie's ex-husband, the three kids had plenty of care. Katie noticed that Franklin seemed upset having the kids at her house, but she figured it was just because he wanted to spend more time with her. Today, Katie had all the kids at her house. They played games while waiting on Todd and Valerie to arrive. Franklin wanted her to tell them their plans as soon as they arrived, but she thought it would be best to wait a day or two and allow them relax after the long trip.

Todd and Valerie arrived and the kids were excited to hear about their honeymoon. They both shared stories of their time away.

"Sounds like you had a great time, I'm so happy for you," Katie said as she hugged Valerie.

"We did, and thank you again for helping to watch my babies," Valerie replied.

Franklin had sat quietly for most of the visit. He laughed when the others laughed and repeated an "oh my" or "wow" when appropriate. He could not wait any longer. "Well, Katie and I have some news for you," he said as he deliberately restrained from looking at Katie. He now had Todd and Valerie's full attention. "We are going to Vegas in a couple of weeks," he smiled widely.

"Vegas," Todd repeated as he looked at Katie.

Katie cleared her throat, "Yes, Franklin wants me to meet his family, and I have never been on a real vacation or even left the state," she offered feebly.

Valerie could sense that her husband was not happy about the news. In an attempt to calm him, she placed her hand on his shoulder and offered a silent prayer for wisdom. "Did you need us to help watch the kids?" she asked.

"No, actually we are taking them with us," she told them.

There was more discussion concerning the trip as well as the newlyweds honeymoon. Once everyone left Katie inquired of Franklin as to why he did not wait, as she wanted. He offered an apology stating that he was excited to share their news.

Katie allowed the women to take a break before continuing. She wanted to talk to Heather about the remaining sessions. She was not sure she could get the rest of what she wanted to say done in two sessions. Heather understood and suggested adding one additional day. They would still have time to make plans for their retreat. When the break was over, Katie told them the change in her testimony dates and continued with her story.

"Franklin's family was awesome, I truly liked them all and they treated me wonderfully."

Katie was apprehensive about meeting Franklin's family. She was not sure what to expect. He did not talk about them much, but when he did, she got the feeling they were very wealthy. They arrived at the airport with two very tired children. Franklin's parents, Forester and Sylvia Harness, waited for them by the gates. After introductions, Sylvia suggested grabbing a bite to eat somewhere before making the trip home. During their meal, Sylvia and Katie chatted about the flight, the children and Katie answered many questions about her family. Forester suggested making a stop on their way home to show Katie and the kids some of the beautiful scenery.

As they drove, his parents told her about the winery. Sylvia's great grandfather started the winery ninety years ago. The winery has been owned and operated by the family since and now is owned and operated by Sylvia and her brother. The winery included a resort and restaurant that offered activities all year. Forester explained that their three children, Franklin and his brother and sister would become owners in the near future.

The estate was larger than anything Katie had ever seen. It reminded her of something you would see in the movies. The long drive leading to the estate was lined with trees. A large fountain was on display in the center of the round parking area in front of the estate. Katie thought it was beautiful. She was surprised to learn that Sylvia did not employee anyone to clean or cook. Sylvia liked to tend to the house herself.

Franklin showed Katie the room for the kids to share and then showed her the room they would share. Embarrassed, she explained to him that she did not feel right sharing a room with him since they were not married and it was his parent's house. Franklin reluctantly agreed. The next few days included the grand tour and lessons on how to grow grapes in a desert. She met the entire family and found they were all very nice.

Katie worried about arriving back in Iowa. She thought about how to break the news to her brother. Would he be mad at her and tell her how irresponsible she was. Franklin did not share her concern and tried to reassure her by telling her they would be happy. He told her it was time for her to have a life of her own. She hoped he was right and agreed with him that it was time for her to have a new life.

Todd and Valerie pulled into the driveway. It had been three weeks since they had last seen Katie and the kids. Katie invited them over for dinner and planned to break the news to them. Katie had already talked to them both on the phone and told them all about their trip, the winery and about Franklin's family. Franklin told her it was time to tell them and asked for everyone's attention.

"Franklin and I got married," Katie said quickly.

Todd and Valerie sat silently for a couple of minutes neither of them knew what to say. Finally, Valerie broke the silence "Congratulations."

Katie told them how she and Franklin took a trip to the Vegas strip and decided to get married while they were there. What she did not tell them was she was drunk and did not remember the wedding until the next morning. Franklin told them their plans to move to his parent's home in April.

Todd finally found his voice, "April!" he said abruptly and then stood up. "Don't you think you are moving a little quick?" He stammered, "Getting married to someone you haven't even dated that long and now moving across the country!" He was furious.

Katie was surprised at his reaction and looked to Franklin for support. Franklin's anger matched Todd's, "Now wait a minute Todd," he snapped. "Katie is an adult and this is her life and mine," he barked back.

Both men now stood toe to toe and Katie feared there was about to be a fight. She was angry and hurt. "Stop!" she hissed "Todd, Franklin is right, this is our life, it is time for me to have a life and that's that." she looked at Valerie. "I hoped you would be happy for us, but apparently you're only happy if you are controlling me." She closed her eyes and suddenly regretted her harsh words. She had never spoken to her brother with such anger before.

"Unfortunately," she told the women, "that was when I stopped talking to my brother." She looked at the back of the room where he sat and again told him how sorry she was for the things that she said. "We moved in April without saying goodbye and didn't talk to anyone again for three long years." She wiped away the tears and told the women she would tell them more at their next meeting.

# Chapter Eight

Katie finished getting the last of the sack lunches made for the kids. "Don't forget no one will be here when you get home from school tonight," she told them. She bent over to kiss Danie's head, "I will see you tonight." She did not try to kiss Roberts head; he told her a year ago he was too old for mom kisses. Once they were loaded on the bus she gathered her bags and headed for orientation. She was excited and nervous at the same time. Excited to be working again and nervous to learn a new job.

She pulled into an open spot and headed toward the front entrance of the clinic. As she walked, she thought she heard someone calling her name. She looked around and spotted Tina coming toward her. Tina told her she had gone to college and was now a dentist and worked on the second floor of the clinic. She asked about the kids and suggested they grab lunch once she had settled into a routine at work.

Katie sat down in the large room and looked around at the other people waiting for the orientation to begin. A few of them were chatting about how boring orientations were and they would be glad when it was over. Katie smiled and thought to herself how right they were. The first three hours were long and drawn out. She shifted several times in her seat and was relieved when they could take an

*Katie's Story*

hour lunch. She sent a text to Tim telling him how boring the meeting was. She walked around the clinic and stopped to see what was going on in the office where she would be working. At the end of the day, she was ready to do anything but sit.

When she got home all five of the kids was watching television. She did not question if they did their homework first. Danie ran to her and told her all about her day at school. Robert chimed in to tell how Danie and another girl have a crush on a boy on their school bus. Danie denied it and told him to be quiet.

"How was work mom?" Robert asked with real interest.

"Long and boring," she told him. "The world of adults, be thankful you're still young."

"Boring, why?" he questioned.

She explained the videos and lectures and how sitting all day was hard to do. He listened, but she could tell he did not fully understand. She thought about how he must feel sitting in class all day.

Danie stumbled over holding her tummy, "what's for supper mom." As long as Katie could remember, whenever Danie was hungry she would rub her tummy as if to say she was starving.

"Meatloaf," she announced and headed toward the kitchen. As she prepared supper she thought about the first time she made meatloaf for Franklin.

Franklin brought in the remaining boxes from his parents estate. They were moving from the big house to a guest house on the back of the property. Franklin thought they needed their own space and privacy.

The guesthouse was large and beautiful. The top floor had four bedrooms and three baths. The main floor had a large living room with vaulted ceilings and a large stone fireplace. A study was located off of the living room as was a half bath. The kitchen was small, but had a large walk-in pantry. She couldn't help but think of how hard it was going to be to keep up with a large house and two kids. She was busy getting supper ready when Franklin walked in.

"What's for supper?" he asked.

"Meatloaf," she replied.

"Oh, meatloaf," he said as he walked past her and placed the boxes in the pantry

"What oh?" she asked jokingly.

"I don't like meatloaf," he drawled his words out and glared at her, "and don't be sarcastic with me," he ordered and walked out the door.

She watched him leave then looked at the bowl of meat wondering what she could make with the hamburger. She had already put eggs and bread crumbs in the mixture. Finally, she went to the pantry and pulled out some garlic and parmesan cheese. Spaghetti and meatballs she told herself. She wondered what was wrong with her husband. He seemed distracted and angry for the last couple of weeks. She thought back to how she responded to him and wondered if perhaps she was out of line. She was just trying to have some fun, she thought to herself.

That night when she served the spaghetti and meatballs Franklin told her he did not care for meatballs either and suggested she take cooking lessons from his mom. She recalled how she was hurt, but could not find the words to say anything. Robert announced he liked meatballs, Franklin ordered him to be quiet while at the table. "Kids are to be seen and not heard, especially when the adults are trying to talk," he scolded.

The sound of Valerie and Todd coming in brought her back to task. She liked meatloaf she thought to herself. Valerie came in and started getting the salad ready. As they prepared supper, Katie told her about her day of orientation and about running into Tina.

After supper, Katie told her about her attempt to make meatloaf for Franklin.

"Wow!" Valerie replied, "Did you take cooking lessons then?"

"Yes and no, I asked his mom for some recipes of foods that he liked." She sat back in her seat and hugged the throw pillow. "Sylvia was always good to me, she knew Franklin gave me a hard time and she really tried to make up for it."

"You're lucky she understood some parents would not." Valerie told her.

"She called yesterday," Katie confided.

"Sylvia called," she asked surprised "Why?"

"She told me that Franklin thought I was in town." She looked around to make sure Robert and Danie were not within earshot. "She doesn't think he will come here, but she wanted me to know."

"Why didn't you tell us?"

"She called late last night, you two were in bed and you were both gone this morning early."

Todd walked in the room and could tell that Valerie was upset. "Trouble?" he questioned.

Katie explained the phone call she received and told them she was not worried about it and they should not worry either. She reasoned that he would not want to show his face here after all that he put her and the kids through.

Todd was not satisfied and thought they still needed to talk. "We will talk about this more later, right now, the kids are coming," he said. Each night the family would sit together in the living room and discuss their day. The kids would tell about their day at school including what they learned and anything else that they wanted to share. The adults then would tell them about their day. Todd would read from the family Bible and then they prayed about what was on their minds.

Robert waited for everyone to tell about his or her day before he told about his. He told them about a boy in his class who had a black eye. He said he had come to school with bruises before and always has a crazy story as to what happened. "I think he is being abused," Robert said matter-of-factly. "Mom, do you remember when you would lie to someone to cover for Franklin, that is what I think he is doing," he looked down at his feet "Sorry mom," he whispered.

Katie could not speak at first. She knew Robert knew what was going on with her and Franklin, but she did not think he caught on to her lies. She thought about the first time she told one of her fibs to cover for him. Franklin was angry because the young man who took her groceries to the car was overly friendly. Katie had laughed it off and made a comment about the age of the kid and Franklin backhanded her. She told everyone she slipped as she got in the car and hit her head on the steering wheel.

"Robert, I know you and Danie seen a lot and I am so sorry. I don't ever want you to apologize, none of what happened was your fault or Danie's fault," she told him.

"What is his name?" Todd questioned.

"It's Luke Barns, I brought him to church one night remember?"

Todd did remember Luke. He asked Robert to tell him more about the kid and other stories that he told them. He decided he would talk to the school counselor and see if there was any way they could get involved. He told Robert how proud he was to have recognized that someone might need help. Together they prayed for his friend's safety.

"Mom, next week we have to give a report on what we want to be when we grow up," Robert told her. "Can you come, with your job, will they care?"

"Sure I'll come; I'll talk to them tomorrow. So, what do you want to be?" she asked.

"You have to wait until next week," he said smiling.

After the kids were in bed, the three adults continued to discuss Franklin and Robert's response. Katie spent some time crying and worrying about the kids. "I know they seen too much, I should have known better," she said. "What has this done to them?" she cried. Todd pointed out that she took the steps she needed to and that he thought both of the kids would be fine. He told her to continue to lead them in the way that they should go and to give them wholly to God.

"I am more concerned right now about Franklin," Todd told her. "What if he comes back here looking for you?"

"I worry too, Katie," Valerie said with a shudder.

"I really don't think he will," Katie said. "I can't imagine after all this time he would come for me."

Todd still was not convinced and insisted that everyone take precautions. He wanted them to be more vigilant of their surroundings and to lock all doors even when home. Valerie agreed and added that they should make sure to tell each other when they will be leaving and where they are going. Katie still thought they were going overboard, but agreed.

# Chapter Nine

Katie was glad that the two days of orientation were complete. Today she would be working in the clinic and learning her job duties. She enjoyed hands on training more than sitting in a chair and taking notes. Cassondra was training her to be Dr. Alderson's nurse. Katie was glad it was Cassondra training her, especially since it was her position she was taking over. She worried about asking for a couple of hours off for the following Monday, but she really wanted to go to the school for Robert's report. When she asked, Cassondra did not hesitate to tell her yes and even added that her children should always come first. After work, she went home and prepared for the nights single mother session.

Heather explained that tonight and the next two sessions would be the final sessions for Katie to speak. She added that both nights Katie would give her testimony and after their break, they would be working on the retreat plans.

Katie greeted the women, "I could take a lot more of your time and tell you each and every little detail concerning my marriage with Franklin, but, I will skip right to the hardest part and go from there," Katie told them.

Katie spent a lot of time with Franklin's mother. She liked Sylvia and enjoyed her company. Today they worked on making cookies for a local homeless shelter. Sylvia volunteered for several shelters in the area, anything from animal to human. Katie enjoyed helping her out and felt good about helping. One of Sylvia's friends offered to watch the children that day which made baking the cookies easier. They were just about finished with the cookies when one of the winery employees ran through the door.

"Sylvia, we need medical, Jessie has been hurt," he said quickly.

Sylvia and Katie quickly followed him out the door. When they arrived, Jessie was holding his hand, which he had wrapped in his shirt. Sylvia began asking what happened and Katie jumped right in and removed the shirt to see how bad the injury was. She turned and looked at Sylvia.

"It's a pretty deep cut, he needs to go to the hospital," she glanced around and spotted a first aid kit on the wall. Directing Jessie to sit down she had one of the men bring her the kit. She wrapped his hand, held it in the air, and applied pressure to the wound. "This will slow and hopefully stop the bleeding, but we need to get him in." She looked at Jessie and told him he was going to need stitches. When one of the other workers appeared with the truck, she told Jessie to keep his arm up and continue to apply pressure. She quickly told the driver the signs of shock and what to do. Another employee went with them just in case they needed his help.

As the women walked back to the house, Sylvia marveled at how Katie was calm and knew exactly what to do. Katie explained to her that she worked as a nursing assistant and had taken training in emergency first aid and CPR. She also told her how she always wanted to be a nurse, but never pursued the training after Robert was born. Sylvia told her she should go to college and get her nursing training adding that she would make a great nurse.

Later that night, Katie told Franklin what happened and what Sylvia said. Franklin told her he already heard and that his mother mentioned that she should go to school.

"Well, what do you think?" she asked.

"About what?"

"School, can I go?"

"I don't think it's a good idea, I think you need to just stay here and make sure you keep the house running smoothly," he told her without looking up from his paper.

"If its money, I'm sure I can get work as a nursing assistant and…"

"No!" he hissed and stood up, "Subject over!"

As she cleaned the dishes, she thought about how much she would have liked to go to school. She thought about his words, "keep things running smoothly," she said to herself.

The next day she did not feel well. She thought she might be coming down with something. She called Sylvia and told her she would not be joining her today. She started to clean the house, but did not feel much like doing anything. She was sitting on the sofa sipping hot tea when Franklin came in.

"Why are you here?" he demanded, "I thought you were going to moms."

"I'm not feeling well, so I thought I would stay in," she said.

"What's wrong, headache, stomach?"

"My stomach is upset and I feel tired," she told him.

He looked at her for a few minutes then headed toward the door. "Well don't sit around all day, the laundry needs to be done today."

She did the laundry and was about to figure out what to serve for supper when Sylvia arrived. She brought chicken soup and bread with her. Sylvia told her she was heading to the store and wanted to know if she needed anything. Katie did have a couple of things she needed, but only one thing she wanted to get right away. She told Sylvia what she wanted and asked her to keep it their secret for a little while.

Katie put the kids to bed early that night and turned in early herself. The next morning her fears confirmed, "Pregnant," she whispered. She promised Sylvia she would let her know as soon as she found out. She sat on the foot of the bed for a long time. This was not what she needed right now, not with her and Franklin fighting all the time. When she thought about it they did not really fight, he did and she simply took it. They had barely been married a year and a half and it was like a prison sentence for her.

She wanted to call Todd and talk to him. There were several times she wanted to call him but did not. She felt guilty about how they left and she did not want to hear an "I told you so." Franklin did not seem to care much for children either; she tried to keep them away from him whenever possible.

She gathered up the kids and headed to the estate. Sylvia was excited and promised not to say anything to anyone. Katie told her she still had not told Franklin and wanted her to act surprised. That night she told Franklin. He did not say anything, he just got in his car and left. When he returned it was after midnight and he was drunk.

Franklin waited a full month before he told his parents. Sylvia talked to Katie about her morning sickness, but she did not tell Forester. When Franklin finally told his parents, he did not show any excitement or enthusiasm an expectant father would show. During the next two months, Franklin was cold toward her. He was upset when she said she needed to go get some new clothes because she was already showing a little bump. He was upset when she did not feel well. He would become irate when she did not get the house cleaned or their meal was not on the table the moment he walked in the door.

Sylvia arrived one afternoon with a truck full of furniture. She bought a crib, a changing table and a basinet. She said she did not purchase clothing since they did not know if it was a girl or a boy. Katie thanked her and invited her to come in for some tea.

"Is Franklin getting better about the baby?" Sylvia asked.

"No," she said softly, "You know?"

"I know my son," she said and took Katie's hand. "I don't understand why he is angry, jealous, and so self-centered," she shrugged her shoulders, "he was not raised that way."

Katie looked at her and realized that she had tears in her eyes. How hard this must be for her. She is excited to have a grandchild and her son does not share in that excitement and joy. Katie realized at that moment that she did not even feel the excitement she should have been feeling. She was fearful and she did not take time to be thankful for the life that was growing inside of her.

"Well," Katie said as she stood up, "grandma, we have some furniture to put together and plans to make. I'm guessing we need to begin to work on a baby shower invitation list." She patted her belly, "I wonder if this will be a boy or a girl." They laughed and talked about funny things children do as they put the furniture together.

Franklin did not say a word when he got home and looked at the furniture set up in the baby's room. After supper that night, Katie asked him if they should begin to discuss baby names. She asked if he had any family names that he would like used.

"Stop!" he said, "I'm tired of hearing about the baby, ok."

The next morning when Katie woke up, he was already gone. Since he was gone, she did not have to make a large breakfast for him. She took her shower and peeked in on the kids. Since they were still sleeping, she decided to enjoy the peace and quiet with the morning paper. She put on her robe and headed down the stairs. Before she realized what was happening, she was lying at the foot of the steps. She lay there for what seemed to be a long time. She felt something wet trickle on her cheek. She was bleeding. When she tried to stand up she felt a sharp pain in her abdomen. Fear and panic set in. She yelled for Franklin then remembered he was not home. She fumbled around and found her cell phone in her robe pocket. She called Sylvia. As she waited for Sylvia to arrive, she looked around her and discovered one of Robert's cars and put it in her pocket.

Sylvia and Forester drove her to the hospital. They tried to call Franklin, but he did not answer the phone. Forester waited in the lobby with the kids and Sylvia stayed with Katie. She had to have a couple of stitches on her eyebrow. The doctor ordered an ultrasound to check on the baby. Katie was worried. She was cramping and felt in her heart that something was wrong. The doctor confirmed her fear that she had lost the baby. Sylvia tried to comfort Katie and wondered where her son was.

Katie sat silently in the back seat of the car as they drove back to the estate. They still had not been able to reach Franklin and Sylvia insisted Katie and the kids stay at their place until he arrived. Katie agreed but for different reasons. Once they arrived, Katie asked Forester if she could have a few minutes to talk to Sylvia alone. She told Sylvia about Franklin's angry outburst the night before. Then she pulled the car out of her purse. "This was what I slipped on," she said holding it out to her. "I know this was not on the floor when we went to bed, and Robert didn't get up in the night," she said flatly.

"Are you sure?" Sylvia gasped.

"Yes, I put the kids to bed early and all the toys were picked up, Franklin went to bed before I did." She looked at the car and tears started to flow down her cheeks, "I would have seen this when I walked up the stairs to go to bed."

"Oh Katie, I don't know what to say or think."

"This morning Franklin left the house early, he didn't wake me up, and he always wakes me up and tells me what he wants for breakfast." She shook her head and placed her hands over her face, "I know he put that car there."

Forester had suspected something was wrong when they could not reach Franklin. He knew that Franklin was not happy about the baby and that his son had not treated his wife the way he should. He was sure that what Katie and his wife were talking about had something to do with his son and he was positive it was not going to be good. He walked into the room to two crying women.

"I want to know what's going on, what he has done this time?" he asked.

Sylvia told him all that had gone on over the past months and what Katie had just told her. Forester was angry. He apologized to Katie and told Sylvia that Katie was to move back in with them that night.

"We will go to the house and get her and the kids clothes for a couple of nights and get the rest later," he said.

Franklin did not get home until after midnight and was drunk. He did not call Katie or return his parent's call. He did not even go to the estate; he went home and went to bed. The next morning he went to get his wife. When he arrived, his parents and Katie sat at the table. Katie was the first to speak.

"Yesterday was the last straw," Franklin started to interrupt, but somehow Katie found the courage to not allow an interruption. "I'm not done Franklin!" she snapped, "I have put up with a lot over the last almost two years. I have allowed you to mistreat my children.

To mistreat me and to control everything." She wiped the tears from her eyes and squared her shoulders. She was sure she would not have been so brave if his parents were not there to support her. "You caused this, my baby, our baby, I, I, I'm leaving. I am filing for a divorce. Do not ever try to contact me or I will have your arrested." At that, she walked out the door and to the room where Franklin's sister was entertaining the kids.

Katie took a deep breath as she looked around the room. Valerie and Todd knew about the loss of her baby, but Tim did not. She could see he was shocked and like the others was wiping away tears. Heather came to the front and dismissed everyone for a break. She reminded them that the second half of the session they would be working on the plans for the retreat.

As Katie drove home from the meeting she could feel that old familiar pain. She wondered if she would see her baby in heaven. She thought about the months that followed the loss of her baby and how she had nightmares. "Does the pain ever really go away?" she asked God as she drove.

# Chapter Ten

The kids were getting their backpacks when Robert asked his mom if he could bring a friend home to study. Todd was planning to pick them up after school so Katie told Robert it was up to Todd. She also said if Todd agreed that she or Todd would need to talk to one of his parents first. When Robert told her it was Luke, she looked at her brother. Todd thought it was a good idea. He told her that yesterday he had gone to the school to talk to the counselor and they were going to keep an eye on him. He thought it would be good for Luke to be around people he could trust.

Cassondra and Katie planned to work late tonight to go over a few files. Katie liked Cassondra and wondered if she were a Christian. The morning was extremely busy and the girls did not have a chance to talk. The doctor was going to be gone after lunch, which would give them more time to go over the files and relax some.

"Wow, what a morning!" Katie said as she collapsed in the chair.

"Some days it is really crazy busy, you'll get used to it," Cassondra said and sat next to her. "How was group last night?"

"Good, it's hard to tell my story sometimes."

"I bet it is. One of the girls from your group is a friend of mine, she told me about you," Cassondra admitted.

*Katie's Story*

Surprised, Katie asked who it was. She told her the girl's name, but Katie did not know who it was. Several women started coming to the group just for the testimony.

"I am a single mom, one kid, her name is Holly, she is eleven," Cassondra told her. "My story is not as important as your story."

"Oh, Cassondra, everyone's story is important, it's a part of the chapter in your life," Katie explained.

"Well, maybe so, but I am the one at fault for my being in this position." Cassondra told Katie how she and her husband started pulling apart in their relationship. They worked many hours and did not see each other much. She told her how during her pregnancy she gained a lot of weight. She admitted that her husband never made comments to her about her weight, but she was not happy. She lost a lot of weight and started going out with her friends. Then she started having an affair with her husband's friend. "That ended our marriage, and their friendship."

"How long have you been divorced?" Katie asked.

"Three years, he is married again and happy," she replied "and, I found forgiveness through Christ. I know he has forgiven me, but I sometimes wonder why."

"Forgiveness is easy to receive, but hard for us to except," Katie admitted. "It took me a little while to get to that point. I know I have forgiven Franklin, but I don't want to ever be around him again."

They got back to work, but continued to talk. Katie told her about her decision to leave Franklin and about her decision to go to college.

Katie and Sylvia sat at the kitchen table and discussed what the next steps would be. Katie told her how she had ended her relationship with her brother and did not want to return home to face him yet. She thought she would find an apartment and apply for a position as a nursing assistant. Forester was listening to Katie; he asked her if she wanted to become a nurse. Katie thought eventually she would, but she did not think she could afford that right away. They insisted she stay with them until she could find a place to live and a job. They felt bad about their son's behavior and truly cared for Katie and the kids. Forester handed her keys to one of their cars and told her to use it as long as she needed. In the meantime, they told Franklin not to bother Katie.

Katie applied at several places before she finally found a place to work. Her nursing assistant certificate was expired so she had to take classes in Nevada. One facility offered to allow her to work and they would provide the training for her. Two months later Katie had enough money to move into an apartment. Because she was a single mother, she was able to get assistance to help her afford a place to live. She did not like to take handouts, but felt that she needed the support until she could get on her feet. Sylvia watched the kids for her while she was at work and helped her locate a regular babysitter.

Katie was heading to the daycare center to pick up the kids. She had not heard from or seen Franklin since that night. The divorce papers were filed and they both signed them. They had a waiting period to go through then it would be final. When she arrived home, Franklin was waiting for her outside of her apartment. Fear gripped her and she would not get out of her car. He walked over to the car and asked if they could talk. He told her he could change and that he was sorry. Katie told him no and drove away. She did not know at first where to go. She did not want to intrude on his parents; she felt they had already done too much for her. She drove around for a while then pulled into a fast food restaurant. After they ate, she drove home and circled the block several times to make sure he was not around.

The next day she told one of her co-workers what happened. The charge nurse heard them talking, and told Katie she needed to put a restraining order on Franklin and to tell his parent's. During her morning break the director of nursing asked her to stop in later and talk to her. She was nervous, thinking she was going to be let go. She had not done anything wrong and her charge nurse told her often that she was a prime candidate to take nursing training. When she walked into her office, she could feel her heart racing.

"Have a seat Katie," she said. Katie sat down and waited. "I have talked to the staff and have learned that you are having problems with Franklin."

Katie was not sure how to answer. She feared she was going to receive a warning for bringing her problems to work. "Yes ma'am."

"Relax you're not in trouble. I happen to be friends with Sylvia," she began. "I have also been told you want to take the nursing program."

Katie confirmed her desire to be a nurse. They discussed several options and Katie left that day feeling as if a weigh had been lifted from her shoulders. She was excited and could not wait to begin her new life. She called Sylvia to tell her what was going on. The facility had a program that paid for some of the cost for college. Because Katie had not been an employee long enough to qualify, they could not offer assistance right away. Additionally, they wanted her to transfer to one of their other locations in California.

Sylvia listened and did not let on as if she knew anything. She asked if she could come over and bring some things she picked up for the kids. They planned to get together the next day since it was her day off work.

Sylvia arrived at noon and brought pizza and gifts. When lunch was over, she told Katie she had a confession to make. Sylvia told her she knew Franklin had been to the apartment. She feared for her safety so she contacted her friend, the director of nursing, and the two of them hatched a plan. Forester was the only other person who knew what was going on. They had good friends in California that Franklin did not know.

Sylvia and Forester helped in locating a place for Katie and the kids to live. They said they would help her move to California, introduce them, and help get them settled. Katie was overwhelmed by their generosity.

The transfer was complete and they headed to California. Forester had arranged for Franklin to be in Vegas for training. When they arrived, Sylvia introduced her to Tony and Debbie Tullis, who happened to be ministers. The church owned several houses in the area that they used to help people in the community who were homeless. It was furnished and the rent was $400 a month, which included all utilities. The minister had also arranged childcare. She would not start her new job for a couple of weeks; therefore, she had time to unpack and get to know the area.

"We have one more surprise for you," Sylvia said and she asked Forester to explain.

"We have given Tony a check to take care of your school for the first year," he said.

"Oh, I can't let you do that!" Katie was in tears.

"Oh yes you can!" Sylvia said and hugged Katie.

"We love you, we want to help," Sylvia told her. "You have to work for a year before they will pay any tuition assistance, so we want to make sure your first year is taken care of so you can concentrate on your studies."

Cassondra was astonished that his parents would do so much for her. Katie agreed that it was definitely something she did not expect and told her that she and Sylvia still keep in contact. The entire time she lived in California, Franklin never found out. She completed her training and in the end worked as a registered nurse.

# Chapter Eleven

Katie wondered how it was going at the house with Luke there. She called Valerie to see if she needed to stop at the store for anything other than bread and milk. Valerie said the boys were in the bedroom working on their reports for what they wanted to be when they grew up. Katie hoped that the school would follow through with trying to determine if he needed help and get it for him. She knew what abuse was like for her and the mental abuse her kids suffered, but this young child endured physical and mental abuse.

Danie greeted her at the door full of stories about her day at school. Katie stuck her head in the door and said hi to Robert, Ronny and Luke, but did not bother them long as they were busy working on their reports. She told Valerie about her day at work and her conversation with Cassandra.

"Where is Todd?" Katie asked.

"Oh, he is in the barn, he needed to make a call and didn't want anyone to hear him," then she nodded toward the room the boys were in.

April and Susan were busy going through their clothes. They had a growing spurt and now needed new clothes. They put the clothing that did not fit them in boxes. Danie was in the middle trying on their clothes hoping that some of them would fit. The boys were taking a break from their reports and wanted to know what was for supper.

"Walking tacos," Valerie smiled knowing they would all be excited, "how are the reports coming along," she asked.

They told her fine and declined to tell what they wanted to be when they grew up. They insisted it was to be a surprise. Luke did not care if they knew so he announced proudly that he wanted to be a firefighter. He told them how his grandfather was a firefighter and he wanted to be just like him. When questioned, he told them that his grandparents lived in Florida, they moved there after he retired. It had been two years since he seen them, but they called each week. Katie could tell that Luke really loved and missed his grandparents. She made a mental note to share that information with Todd.

Supper was done and Todd was going to take Luke home. Robert and Ronny wanted to go along. Valerie asked the boys to carry the boxes of clothing to her van so she could take them to town the next day. After they left, Katie and Valerie discussed Luke. Valerie told her that the teacher called and they believed his father abused him. Since Luke would not talk to the counselor, they hoped that Todd or Robert could learn anything they could from Luke. The counselor would be taking action the following week. Katie thought they should tell Todd right away about Luke's grandparents and prayed they would take Luke.

When Todd returned he told them that he was able to talk with Luke alone. He said he asked him if he was having problems at home and needed to talk to someone. Luke didn't want to talk at first then eventually opened up and told Todd what had been going on. He was afraid that his father would find out that he talked to someone. Todd told Luke that his father would not find anything out, at least not right away. He explained that he had contacted the school and wanted to help. He prayed with Luke and asked God to protect him.

Todd was glad to hear about Luke's grandparents and thought he would call the counselor and tell him right away. As he made the call, Katie and Valerie talked to the boys and asked them not to say anything to Luke. They explained that at this point they were trying to be very careful in order to protect Luke from retaliation. When Todd got off the phone, they held their nightly gathering and prayed. Danie prayed that she could get a new puppy; the twins prayed that someone would get good use from their clothing, and the boys prayed for Luke.

On Monday morning, the boys were excited about their reports. Instead of taking the bus, they would all go together to the school. Even though the reports would not start until 9:30, Todd wanted to talk more with the counselor. The counselor had good news. They had contacted the grandparents and told them what was going on. Luke's mother had passed away several years ago, leaving Luke with his father. Her parents were the grandparents that Luke was close too. The grandparents arrived on Sunday night and picked up Luke. Luke's father was facing charges. The counselor told them that Luke took everything well and that he was at school that day because he wanted his grandparents to hear his report. Luke would be the first student to give his report. His grandparents were staying at Luke's house with Luke until the end of the week then they would leave for Florida.

Katie and Valerie could not contain their tears as Luke gave his report. He told the class about his grandparents. His grandpa took him for rides on the fire truck when he was younger. He told the class about the meals the firefighters would cook, adding that they were good cooks. He told the class about the time his grandfather saved the life of a little boy trapped in a burning house. Without warning, he looked at his grandpa and told him thank you for now saving his life. His grandparents could no longer hold back their tears.

When it was Ronny's turn to give his report, he told the class about his favorite teacher, Mr. Northrop. Ronny told how his teacher helped him when he needed help and how he always seemed to like teaching. Ronny announced that when he graduated high school he fully intended on going to school to become a teacher. Valerie and Todd were very proud. His father was there that day and commented to Todd and Valerie that he thought that was a good choice.

It was now time for Robert's report. He walked to the front of the room and began his report. "In my bible there is a verse that I want to read," he looked at the teacher to see if she would say anything, when she did not he opened his Bible and read [8]"Proverbs 22:6. Train up a child in the way he should go: and when he is old, he will not depart from it." He put the Bible back down and began to give his speech.

He told his class about his uncle Todd and his faith in God. He told them how his mother moved to Nevada with her husband and how they ended up in California after the divorce. He looked at his mom, "After you changed I could see that you wanted me and Danie to have the best life, and you taught us about the Bible and about God." He did not tell everyone the problems they had, but he shared a couple of stories about his Sunday school teacher and the youth leader at their church. After he told of his experience, he put his papers down. "When I grow up, I will be a preacher. God has called me and I will follow." His words were strong, he spoke with a conviction that told everyone in the room that he had in fact heard from God, and he would be a preacher.

Again, there were many tears. Tim arrived late, but was able to be there for Robert's report. He took Katie's hand and whispered, "I told you he would be fine." The remaining classmates gave their reports, some wanted to be doctors, lawyers, and one little girl wanted to be a dancer. Katie tried to listen to each report, but often found her thoughts going back to the report her son gave. At that moment she was the proudest she had ever been and thankful that she finally got on the right track with her life.

Todd announced a celebration was in order. They would all go out for pizza. He was sure to invite Luke's grandparents and Luke. As they walked to their cars, he looked at his wife and sister, "God sure works in mysterious ways." They did have a celebration that night. Luke's grandfather thanked Todd for his willingness to get involved and help his grandson. They exchanged addresses and phone numbers and promised to keep in touch.

# Chapter Twelve

It was her final night to speak to the single mothers support group. She was humbled by the events of the week and anxious to share her final testimony. Not only did she get to hear her son's announcement that he wanted to be a preacher, but she also found a house.

"Oh I love it," she told Valerie as they walked through the little house. She was able to get a loan, which surprised her, and she thanked God for making it happen. Todd was walking through the house checking to make sure it was in good shape for her. A few things needed repaired, but nothing he and Tim could not handle. It was close to town yet outside of the city limits. "It has three acres of land so I can have a garden and the kids have a lot of room to play," she told Tim. Danie came running in the house with Robert.

"Mom, does this mean I can have that puppy?" she asked breathlessly, "you said if we found a place with a lot of room I could have one." She added wanting to make sure her mother had not forgotten her promise.

"If we get the house, yes, you can have the puppy." She laughed then added in a serious voice "You have to take care of it."

The house was an older cottage style that was nestled by large walnut, oak and elm trees. With four bedrooms and two baths it suited them well. She really liked that the house set back from the gravel road. She loved the yard and was told that wild berries grew along the back fence.

She received approval for the loan on the house and they would begin moving in the following month. Tim and Todd made a list of things that needed fixed before she moved in and Katie and Valerie looked at paint and decided on the colors to use. Everything seemed to be falling into place. Katie again thanked God for all that he had done for her and her family.

Tim and Katie were having a nice quiet dinner. He wanted to take her out to celebrate her home purchase. After dinner, they went for a walk through the park.

"Katie, you know I love you," he said suddenly.

"Yes, I know and I love you too," she said softly.

They continued to walk for a little while then stopped next to a large elm tree. It was a beautiful spot in the park. There was a stone walk the led to a wooden bridge. The bridge arched up in the middle. He took her hand and led her to the bridge. They stopped to look over the side at the creek below. He then got down on one knee and took her hand.

Katie's heart was racing and she felt as if she would collapse. Tears began to flow down her cheeks. She knew she loved Tim, but she was not ready to get married. She wanted to stop him before he said anything, but she was afraid she would hurt him.

"I know I love you," he began; "I also know that it is too soon to ask for your hand in marriage." he spoke softly.

Katie looked at him and blinked back tears. "I, I don't understand." she stumbled over her words.

"I want to date you exclusively and allow God to lead us in the direction he would have us go." He studied her face as he waited for her to reply. It occurred to him that she must have thought he was going to ask her to marry him. He scolded himself for getting down on one knee. "What must she think?" he asked himself.

Katie allowed his words to sink in. She was embarrassed that she thought he was proposing and amazing at how he asked her to go steady with him.

Tears were flowing down her cheeks and she said yes she would date him exclusively. She laughed as he picked her up and twirled her around until they both had to hold on to the bridge railing to control their dizziness. She told him how she was afraid he was going to propose and explained that she loved him, but was also sure they needed to date and allow God to lead them.

She thought to herself, "third times the charm," then smiled and thought, "God, thank you for giving me the perfect man for me. I am sorry I didn't listen to you a long time ago." She took Tim's hand, "So, we are steady," she laughed.

Katie was in her room preparing for the nights session. She was prepared before, but with the changes of the day she needed to update her outline. When they arrived, she asked Valerie and Todd to sit up front with Tim.

"So much has happened this week," she said. "I had a plan for tonight, and then I needed to make a few changes. But first, I want to tell you about when I allowed Christ in my life."

College was a little harder than she thought it would be. She had a full load of classes, worked full time, and had two children to take care of. She was thankful for the Tullis family and for all their help. She made friends with some of the people from the church. She was attending church for almost a full year, she only attended because she felt obligated to do so since the pastors were helping her out. She was on a school break and happy to have a little free time. She also took

*Katie's Story*

a week off work so she could spend extra time with the kids. During her break, the church was holding a revival. At first, she did not plan on going then at the last minute decided to go. Mainly because the kids wanted to go since there were special activities for them to do.

The church was packed, but she was able to find a spot near the front. She usually volunteered to be in the nursery during church service, this way she could avoid any sermons. Since the nursery already had a full staff, she would get a sermon if she wanted it or not. The evangelist wife and kids sang several songs. She enjoyed the music and thought how it would have been nice if she could sing that well. She shifted in her seat a lot when they sang the song [9]"He Touched Me."

The evangelist started his sermon by slowly singing the words of the song they just finished "Shackled by a heavy burden, beneath a load of guilt and shame, then the hand of Jesus touched me, and now I am no longer the same." Again, Katie shifted in her seat. She knew what it was like to be shacked, to feel shame and guilt. She wished the night were over so she could leave.

He started reading from [10]John chapter 4. As he read verse 28 her heart heard every word clearly, so clear that she thought it was Jesus himself speaking to her at that moment. "Then the woman left her water jar and went away to the town. And she began telling the people, Come see a man who has told me everything that I ever did!" The evangelist started to tell about this Samaritan woman at the well. She went to the well for some water and ended up face to face with the Messiah. He told how everyone has a past of rights and wrongs. He talked about how everything we do Jesus see's, but loves us unconditionally during it all. How when he wants to talk to us he sometimes uses others, or situations, or other means in which to get our attention.

She looked around the room and smiled, "That night, I finally stopped running; I knew I was that Samaritan woman. I knew that Jesus was tugging at my heart and it was time to stop running." She wiped a tear away. "Well, actually, I did run, straight to that alter! When they had the alter call I couldn't wait to get there and get cleaned in the living waters!"

She told them how she called Todd and Valerie that night and asked for their forgiveness. She told them what had happened over the past few years. [11]"Like the prodigal son, I was the prodigal sister, and my brother took me back without question."

Looking quickly at her watch she knew she needed to finish up soon. "I told you that this week had been a humbling week for me. The bank approved me for a loan this week and we found a house. We will move in next month. I want to tell you how my week started. On Monday, my son gave a report on what he wanted to be when he grows up. I worried about both of my children. They both have seen and heard so much. I worried about the baggage I had left in their lap." Opening her bible, she read the same scripture Robert did when he started his report. "My son read this to his class without fear of being made fun of. He told his classmates and their parents how God has called him to the ministry and how he will be a preacher and answer that call."

[12]"Jeremiah 33:3 says, Call unto Me and I will answer thee and show thee great and mighty things, which thou knowest not. In the mess that I was in, all it took was for me to Call on Him and he answered me. By his grace, I have been set free. He answered me and by his grace, he has set my children free. He has shown me great and mighty things. He has used my tragedies, the loss of our parents and my husband to bring Todd to meet Tim. His meeting Tim is what led to Todd receiving the forgiveness and grace God offers so freely. He

brought Todd Valerie, who has been a great soul mate for my brother. He has shown me that I can even love again. He showed me today when Tim asked me to go steady, and I said yes!"

She glanced at Todd and Valerie who were crying along with everyone else in the room. "I know that some of you are still hurting and probably running. I know because I did. I ask right now, that if any of you need that same touch from God that I received, that you come on up front. Let us pray for you. Allow Jesus to set you free and to give you a new life."

As she watched, several women left their seats and headed to the front of the room. She felt a renewing of hope. Hope that even a simple forgiven single mother from Iowa could share Gods forgiving grace to other hurting women.

# Katie's Story
## Part Two
## *Renewed Life*

# Chapter One

Katie sat at the dining room table watching out the window. She loved how the leaves changed colors. She missed this when she lived in California. The changing of the seasons was different there. The trees around her house were turning a deep purple, yellow, red and orange. In California, most of the trees that surrounded her just turned brown. She watched as the wind blew the leaves across the yard. She laughed as Tiger, the yellow lab, chased and barked at the leaves. She was reluctant to get the lab at first; she knew it would be a large dog. Now, she loved him as much as she loved her children. He was a great companion for the kids.

She looked at the clock and figured it was time to get busy. She had a stack of thank-you cards that needed filled out and mailed. Picking up her list, she began thoughtfully filling out each one. She felt blessed to have family and friends who took the time to help her furnish her home. She did not have any furniture when she returned to Iowa and now she had a house full. She was amazed how each piece fit with the other furniture. Once the cards were completed, she called for Tiger and headed to the mailbox. She played fetch with him as they headed back to the house. Again, she thought about how much fun it was to have him as part of the family.

Next on her agenda was to search her recipes. She pulled a large shoebox out of the cabinet and placed it on the table. She refilled her coffee cup and lifted the lid off the box of family recipes. Todd and Valerie had given her some recipes, but most of them belonged to her mother and grandmother. This year, she would be preparing the entire Thanksgiving meal for her family, Todd's family and for Tim. In years past, she would make one or two dishes and joined other family gatherings. Never had she been responsible for the entire meal. She wanted it to be perfect. She remembered fondly how her mother and grandmother would spend hours in the kitchen preparing the large feast. Her grandmother's house was always filled with laughter and stories of the past. "I hope I do these recipes justice," she whispered. Once she decided on what to serve, she prepared a grocery list. "Now, the fun part," she said as she placed the box back in the cabinet.

"Come on Tiger," she called as she opened the gate to the pen. "I know you don't like it, but I am pretty sure you are not allowed in the grocery store." Tiger entered the pen and waited. His tail was wagging in anticipation. Sure enough, she pulled out a bone and handed it to him. He no longer cared that he had to be in the pen.

While she waited for the kids to get out of school, she thought she would call Valerie. She did not find a recipe for one of the deserts her aunt always made and wanted to find it.

"Hey Valerie, what's new?" she asked.

"I was just about to call you," she replied. "Where are you?"

"I am at the school waiting for the kids to get out, why?"

"What are you doing after you pick them up?" Valerie asked. Her voice sounded like a schoolgirl with a secret to tell.

"Grocery shopping!" she sighed.

"When you're done, why don't you give me a call and we will bring chicken and sides for everyone."

"Sure," she said and thought how funny she sounded. "Once the torture of shopping is over we would love chicken!"

After the shopping was finished and they returned home, she sent a text to Valerie. It took several trips to unload the car; grocery sacks lined the kitchen counters and the table. As they unpacked the groceries, Katie would direct Robert and Danie as to where to put them.

"My cabinets will not know what to do with this much food," she laughed.

Danie was putting the canned goods in the pantry, "Mom, I don't have homework tonight, when the groceries are put away can I go out and play with Tiger?"

"Sure, be sure to give him some fresh water and feed him," she told her happy daughter. She knew she did not have to remind her to feed and water him; both of the kids did a great job caring for him.

Robert went to his room and Danie was out back playing with Tiger. Katie sat at the table reviewing her grocery list. She discovered she forgot a few important items. She made a note to go back to the store on her way home from work on Monday. The sound of Tiger's barking alerted her that their company had just arrived. She went to meet them at the door. Tiger enthusiastically greeted them, wagging his tail, barking and bouncing around them. Katie noticed how he calmed down when greeting Todd. She wondered if he sensed that Todd had a prosthetic leg and did not want to hurt him. Ronny rushed past her to find Robert, and April and Susan to find Danie.

Valerie was carrying a bag and Todd had the chicken. "Come on in, put it on the table and I will get dishes and napkins," Katie told them. When she turned around, she noticed the large smile on

Todd's face. "Good grief, what's up with you?" she asked as she put the plates on the table. Sitting on the table was a gift-wrapped box with her name on it. She looked at Todd then at Valerie.

"Well, open the box." Todd said.

"What is it? It's not my birthday," she said as she looked at Valerie.

"Just open the box!" Valerie told her.

She opened the box and found a hand-made booklet inside. On the cover it read, "God is Good All the Time!" She opened the booklet and read the contents.

> [13]So Hannah ate. Then she pulled herself together, slipped away quietly, and entered the sanctuary. The Priest, Eli, was on duty at the entrance to God's temple in the customary seat. Crushing soul, Hannah prayed to God and cried and cried inconsolably. Oh, God of the Angle Armies, if you'll take a good, hard look at my pain, if you'll quit neglecting me and go into action for me by giving me a son, I'll give him completely, unreservedly, to you. I'll set him apart for a life of holy discipline. It so happened that as she continued in prayer before God, Eli was watching her closely. Hannah was praying in her heart, silently, her lips moved but no sound was heard. Eli jumped to the conclusion that she was drunk. He approached her and said, "You're drunk! How long do you plan to keep this up? Sober up, Woman!" Hannah said, "Oh no, sir, please! I'm a women hard used. I haven't been drinking. Not a drop of wine or beer. The only thing I've been pouring is my heart, pouring it out to

God. Don't for a minute think I'm a bad woman. It's because I'm so desperately unhappy and in such pain that I've stayed here so long." Eli answered her, "Go in peace, and may the God of Israel give you what you have asked of him.

I Samuel 1:9-17

After she finished reading the booklet, she noticed a small wrapped package in the bottom of the box. She opened it to find a rubber ant. She stood silent for a moment then realized what was happening.

"Oh, my, Oh my goodness!" she exclaimed. "A baby, you are having a baby!"

The five kids had walked into the room just as Katie and Valerie started hopping about laughing. Ronny told Robert and Danie what was going on. April and Susan looked at each other and rolled their eyes. Todd was laughing and taking pictures with his cell phone.

Valerie told Katie how they both wanted a baby, but figured that after nine years it just was not going to happen. She told her that she would continue to pray about it, but that she did not dwell on it as she had in the past. Todd explained that recently, they had talked about adopting.

"It was Todd's idea to tell you this way." Valerie told Katie.

"Well, it's sort of like Hannah, except, the preacher is not getting this kid!" Todd laughed, "We should eat before the chicken gets cold."

After everyone left and the kids were in bed Katie sat on the porch with a cup of hot tea. She thought about how happy Todd and Valerie seemed. "A baby," she said softly. "Thank you God, for answering their prayers." She thought about Valerie's age. At thirty-six years, having a baby could be risky. Valerie assured her that the doctor said she was in good health and she and Todd were not worried. She wondered for a while if she and Tim did get married if he wanted children. She thought about having another baby, but at the same time, the thought was scary. "Another bridge for another day," she said as she walked in the house.

# Chapter Two

Katie and Tina sat in the cafeteria talking during their lunch. They talked about the funny things that Robert would say and do when Tina babysat for him.

"I remember when I found the worms he left in his pocket." Tina laughed, "He wanted to keep them warm so they could go fishing." She looked at Katie and instantly felt bad. "I am so sorry. I didn't mean to bring up…"

Katie smiled, "It is okay, we talk about Danny, and he was a large part of our lives and the kid's father." Katie thought back to that day again and remembered that Tina had taken Robert home. Suddenly she realized that although Danny was not around Tina much, she still had a connection with him. She vaguely remembered how upset Tina was when she learned of his death.

Tina looked down at her cup of tea, "I really liked Danny, and he was funny and always very nice to me."

"I know, and he really liked you too," she told her.

They discussed their jobs and Katie told her how much she really liked working in the clinic. She explained that she did not feel as overwhelmed as she had when she first started.

"What are your Thanksgiving plans?" Katie asked.

"We are going to Larry's family this year," she said smiling, "this will be the first for meeting the entire family, I am a bit nervous."

Katie shared with her how nervous she was to meet Franklin's parents. "Turned out I liked them better than I liked Franklin," she added.

Katie told her about her plans and that this year they had even more to be thankful for, with the announcement of a new niece or nephew. She suggested that Tina and Larry come over sometime for dinner and catch up.

"It is difficult to catch up over a thirty minute lunch!" Katie told her. They exchanged phone numbers and called it a date.

The remaining afternoon was busy. Katie could not imagine getting all the people in the waiting room taken care of before closing. She figured they would be late so she sent a text to Robert to let him know. She picked up a file, walked to the door, and called out the name of the next patient. As she glanced around the room, she made eye contact with Rhonda. It took a minute before she recognized her. Smiling she waved and ushered the waiting patient to the back. She did not remember seeing Rhonda's name on the list, but figured she had an appointment with the other doctor.

"Hi Katie," Rhonda said as she passed her in the hall.

"Hi," she stopped and looked at her. She thought she looked older than she should. "How have you been?" she asked with genuine concern.

"Oh, ya know, I have this cold and can't seem to shake it." She said as the nurse opened the examination room door. "Good to see ya." she said as she disappeared behind the door.

At the end of the day, Katie was glad to see the last patient leave. She finished working on some patient files and made a reminder note for things to do the following day. The other nurses were chatting about their plans for the weekend and thanksgiving. Katie wanted to ask about Rhonda and decided she should not. She told herself that it was not her business unless made her business by her boss or Rhonda. Still, she thought, Rhonda looked awful. She finished her work for the night and headed out the door.

As she crossed the parking lot, she could see someone sitting on the curb at the end of the parking lot. As she approached, the figure started moving toward her and she realized who it was. Her heart began beating faster and stronger.

Panicked, she fumbled with her keys and reached for her cell phone. She glanced around the parking lot to see if anyone was around in case she needed help. Her heart was racing and she began to shake. For a minute she thought she should turn and run the other direction but realized it would not do her much good. The figure was now about three feet from her and standing next to her car. She stopped, frozen, not sure what to say or even how to respond.

"Katie," he said, "You look, great!" He took a step toward her then stopped when she took two steps backwards.

"What do you want Franklin?" her voice shaky. She managed to find her phone in the bottom of her purse and now held on to it ready to call for help.

Franklin looked around the parking lot then back to Katie. "I heard you were working here, I just wanted to say hi," he said.

Fear gripped her as she realized he had one hand behind his back. Her heart pounded and she instantly thought he might have a gun. "Would he shoot me?" she asked herself. She could feel sweat run down the side of her face. She prayed silently for God to protect her. She moved slowly backward as he moved his arm. Slowly his elbow appeared, then the cuff of his coat. She dropped her purse and bags on the ground and then put her hands out in front of her as if to fence off the bullet. Her body trembled and she looked at his face. "Evil smile," she thought. He smiled at her and his eyes seemed to pierce right through her body.

Franklin sensed her fear and enjoyed the power he had over his ex-wife. He knew she thought the worse about what he concealed behind his back. Deliberately he stopped to see her reaction. At last, he revealed the hidden object and smiled triumphantly.

Katie caught her breath and her hands dropped to her side. "Flowers!" she said loudly. "You, you have flowers?" She picked up her bag and purse, moved past him, and got in her car. She was no longer afraid but angry. She locked the doors and started the car. When she looked in the rearview mirror, she could see him standing behind her car. "I should run you over," she hissed. Without hesitation, she put the car in reverse, thinking he will move or the car will hit him. Part of her was relieved when he stepped away and she pulled out of the parking lot.

She only drove a couple of blocks then the tears began to flow. She began crying so hard she needed to pull over and regain control. She was angry for being afraid and for still feeling afraid. She looked around the parking lot of the gas station she pulled into. She did not see him there. Nobody seemed to notice she was sitting in her car in the middle of the lot crying. Once she was able to think clear, she pulled into a spot at the station and called Tim.

Tim was instantly angry and told her to stay put that he was on his way. She went inside the station and poured a cup of coffee. She sat at the table looking out the window for any signs of Franklin or Tim. When someone walked behind her, she jumped. She glanced over her shoulder and spotted a couple of small kids looking at her. She could see concern in their eyes and wondered if they sensed something was wrong. She looked from the kids to their mother who was also looking at her. A man came out from the back and the woman handed the kids over to him, she said something quietly to him and then walked toward Katie.

"Honey, I am sure it is none of my business, but are you okay?" the woman asked her "You look as if you have seen a ghost."

Katie cleared her throat. "I'm, yes, I am okay, just a bit shaken up."

"Well, I can tell something is wrong, you don't have to tell me anything." she offered, "I just wanted you to know that for whatever reason, when you walked in here, I prayed for protection for you."

Katie let down her guard and allowed her tears to roll down her face. "Thank you," she accepted a Kleenex and wiped her eye's. "I truly, truly, appreciate it."

"I am assuming you are waiting for someone to come here," the kind woman said.

"Yes, my boyfriend, he should be here any minute."

"Well, we will just wait with you." she said and motioned for her family to come and join them.

"Oh, no, I couldn't impose…"

"Now missy, it is not an imposition, we will wait and chat about something happy." The woman told her as the rest of the family came over and took their seats. She introduced herself and her family and told Katie how they were passing through on their way to Illinois to visit family. "I couldn't imagine why we stopped here, I wanted to stop at a restaurant, but Henry insisted we stop here." She said and smiled as she looked at her husband. "I guess God knew you were in need of some backup."

Tim pulled in the parking lot and ran inside. He did not recognize the people talking with Katie, but in his heart he did not consider them a threat. He walked over and placed a hand on Katie's shoulder.

"Are you okay?" he asked concerned.

Katie stood up, threw her arms around his neck, and told him through sobs what happened, forgetting the family that still sat at the table listening. She turned and apologized to them. They assured her that no apology was necessary and that they would pray for her and left.

Katie told Tim what the woman said to her. They sat for a while talking before he followed her home. When they arrived at the house, Katie was glad to see Todd and Valerie waiting inside. Tim told her he called Todd as they entered the house.

Valerie was the first to run to her, "Are you okay, he didn't hurt you did he?" she questioned as she hugged her tightly.

"No, he didn't touch me." she said and hugged Todd. As she took a seat she told them how he appeared and how she was scared. She told them how he slowly pulled his hand out from behind his back while smiling his evil smile.

"Did he say if he knew where you lived? He knows where you work now!" Todd said as quietly as he could. "What about the kids?" he finished.

"I don't want them involved, it…" she started to say.

"No, Katie, they need to be involved, they have to know he is here so they can watch for him." Tim interjected.

They all agreed that Tim was right and brought the kids in to discuss what had happened. Robert's anger matched that of Todd's. Katie could not help but smile at his protecting nature. Katie refused to leave her home, but did allow Tim to stay in the guestroom. Ronnie, Jacob and Robert declared they would sleep in the living room and keep watch for any activity outside. Danie reminded them that Tiger would let them know if anyone showed up and said they should bring him in for the night. Katie knew this was a ploy to be able to have Tiger in the house, but agreed with the logic and caved in.

Katie tossed and turned during the night. Every sound she heard was louder than she remembered. The wind was blowing hard and the branches rubbed against the back of the house just outside her bedroom window. She prayed and cried for God's help. She looked at the clock and wondered if she would ever fall asleep. She had to go to work the next day. Tim wanted her to call off work, but she did not want to allow Franklin to run her life. She needed to work; she needed to live her life without fear. When she finally fell asleep, it was past one.

# Chapter Three

Katie left the office and headed to her car. She looked around the parking lot as she walked, fearful that Franklin would appear. She reached her car and unlocked the door. Again, she turned to make sure no one was around. She quickly got in the car and slammed the door locking it quickly. Putting the key in the ignition, she adjusted her seat then began to back out of the parking spot. She felt relieved that Franklin was not in the parking lot today. She hoped she did not have to see him again. She rounded the corner and headed toward the south side of town. Just as she reached for the radio dial, she heard something behind her. Looking in the rearview mirror, she could see Franklin's face peering back at her. He reached around the seat and grabbed her shoulders.

"Drive, or else." he demanded.

Scared, Katie screamed.

Robert was the first to burst into her room.

"Mom, mom, are you alright?" He said as he ran to her, Jacob and Ronnie followed on his heels. Tim now entered the room and looked around.

Crying, "It was a dream, he was in the car, he grabbed me!" she sobbed loudly. Tim was now on the side of the bed holding her shaking body. She cried for a few minutes and then embarrassed she looked up at the boys. She could tell how concerned they were for her.

"Mom, I think you should stay home today." Robert told her as he walked to the door to greet Danie.

"What's wrong?" Danie asked and looked sleepily at the boys then at her mom.

"Mom had a bad dream." Robert told her.

It was now six o'clock, and the alarm started with the roster crow announcing it was time to get up and prepare for the day. Tiger had joined the family in Katie's bedroom and made himself known by jumping on the bed to lick the tears from her face. She hugged Tiger and laughed then she pushed him off the bed.

"Nope, I am going to work." she insisted, "Kid's, start getting your morning chores done." She looked at Tim and smiled feebly. "Would you mind taking me to work and picking me up?" He agreed and headed to the kitchen to make some coffee and breakfast.

After everyone had breakfast and was dressed and ready to go, Tim told them all to watch out for each other and if they see Franklin they should go the opposite direction and get help. He then had them all stand in a circle and hold hands. He opened the Bible to [14]Psalm 121 and read "I lift up my eyes to the mountains--where does my help come from? My help comes from the Lord, the maker of heaven and earth. He will not let your foot slip--he who watches over you will not slumber, indeed, he who watches over Israel will neither slumber nor sleep. The Lord watches over you--the Lord is your shade at your right hand, the sun will not harm you by day, nor the moon by night. The Lord will keep you from all harm--he will watch over your life, the Lord will watch over your coming and going both now and forevermore." He then prayed for each one of them.

Todd had tried to call Katie and when she did not answer, he called Tim. He wanted to know how she was and to see if she changed her mind about going to work. Tim told him about her nightmare and confided that he was worried about Franklin's appearing in town. Todd asked Tim to come over once Katie was at work. When Tim arrived, Todd had just hung up the phone with one of his friends who happened to be a police officer.

"I asked Steve if there was anything we could do to keep Franklin from going around any of us." He told Tim as they sat down. Valerie had the day off and brought them some coffee. Todd started to tell about his conversation with Steve.

"What did he say or suggest?" Valerie asked.

"Well, it seems that since there was never a record of abuse, or any sort of court ordered restraining order, there is little we can do." he said exasperated.

"There has to be something we can do." Valerie murmured.

Tim was upset and stood up and looked out the window. "I know what I would like to do!" He said roughly. "But, I know I cannot." He turned and looked at Todd with an expression that said he was not happy. "He better not touch her or the kid's."

They talked about securing the house with different locks and even getting a security camera. Tim wanted everyone to make sure no one went out alone. Todd told them Steve would check to see if he could locate where Franklin was staying and Valerie said she would give Sylvia a call and let her know what was going on.

Katie tried to keep her mind off Franklin. The office was busy so that helped some. As she was placing some files on the counter, she noticed Rhonda's file. "That's it," she said and picked up the file. Stacy, another nurse who worked for the other doctor was standing next to her.

*Katie's Story*

"That's what?" she asked.

"Yesterday, Rhonda was here to see the doctor. She and her boyfriend are friends with Franklin, she called him," she told her. "That has to be it, otherwise, how would he know I worked here?"

"You might be right." Stacy told her.

During Katie's lunch, she called Tim to tell him about Rhonda and what she assumed must have happened. Tim too thought Rhonda must have called Franklin. He was also concerned that no one had any idea how long he had been in town. He told Katie the locks in the house were all changed and Todd and Valerie were going to Des Moines the next day to a security store to pick up security cameras. Katie was sitting on the far side of the cafeteria and did not notice Rhonda was sitting behind her. When she hung up, she sat back in her seat and wondered if Franklin would show up again today. She remembered her nightmare and shuddered. She was deep in thought and did not realize Rhonda now stood next to her.

"Katie," Rhonda said apprehensively.

Katie, startled, just about fell out of her seat. "Rhonda," she said suspiciously.

"Katie, I am sorry," she began as she pulled up a seat and looked around the room. "When Leo picked me up here yesterday I told them I seen you."

"Why would you do that? You know we are divorced."

"I didn't think about it until after I said it." She looked around the room again, but this time Katie noticed.

"Is he here, is that what you're doing is looking for him?" she asked and hastily stood up and looked around.

"No, I am just as nervous as you. I don't trust him, he is weird." She tried to convince her old friend. "I didn't even think about it and I certainly didn't think he would show up and wait for you." She stood up and looked at Katie, "I'm sorry, I just wanted you to know that. Also, he is staying in Fairfield." She turned to walk away then stopped and spoke over her shoulder. "Be careful, he is dangerous and crazy." At that, she walked away.

Katie glanced at her watch and realized she was now ten minutes late returning to work. She rushed through the cafeteria and ran up the stairs. When she walked into the office Stacy could tell Katie was upset so she told her to go to the back room. Katie did and tried to steady her nerves while she waited. Stacy told her that she figured with everything that was going on she would watch out for Rhonda or someone fitting Franklin's description. Monica, a co-worker, spotted Rhonda going into the cafeteria and followed. "She came back from break and told me so I have been covering for you. If you need to take the rest of the day off, leave, we can handle this." She told her. Reluctantly Katie did take the rest of the day off. She could not concentrate on her work and needed to get away.

# Chapter Four

Tim stayed the night again. The next day when Todd and Valerie returned from shopping, they installed the security cameras and tested them. Katie spent most of the day in her room with her door shut. Her mind muddled and she felt as if she were lost in some crazy dream. She did not understand why he would show up after all this time. She tried to call Sylvia, and then remembered that they were going to Honduras on a mission trip and would not return until the middle of December. She figured Franklin thought this would be the best time to show up since his parents were out of the country. She wondered if he knew how much his parents had helped her.

"Katie, are you awake?" She heard Valerie call softly outside the door.

"Yes, come on in," she answered and sat up on her bed pulling the covers up around her neck. "I just don't understand why he is here now. What does he want?" she asked in desperation.

Katie recalled the time in which his parent's helped move her to California. They had sent Franklin to Vegas for training so he would not know what was going on. She remembered that when Sylvia called or when they visited her, they made sure they had good cover stories and Franklin was busy. Even when she sent birthday or holiday card's, she placed Katie's card inside an envelope and sent it to the Tullis family. They would then send the card to Katie. "All the precautions and he still finds out where I am," she told Valerie.

"Okay, that's enough!" Valerie finally told her. "To begin with, where else do you think he would look? You are from Ottumwa; of course he would look here for you." She took hold of Katie's shoulders, "You can't hide in your room." She took Katie's hands and lifted her from the bed. "Now, this is the weekend we were going to go over the Thanksgiving dinner plans and make sure we had everything."

Tim had Robert and Katie go outside and showed them the cameras and how to monitor the activities on her television. Tim said he would head home and clean up and be back later. Katie insisted that he needed to stay at his house, adding how it might look to others if he stayed. She also declined to stay at Todd's house. She explained that she did not plan to leave the house until the next morning for Sunday school and she had plenty to keep her mind busy. She reminded them she offered to teach a Sunday school class and needed to get her ducks in a row to teach. Reluctantly, they agreed and left.

That night, the three of them sat in the living room, read from the Bible, discussed and prayed for things that were heavy on their hearts. Robert received a letter from his friend Luke and said they were coming to Ottumwa in December to visit family. He wanted to invite them over one night to visit. Katie said she would talk to them and make arrangements. She was happy to hear that Luke was doing well.

Danie said she was concerned about April and Susan. She told her mom that they were talking about some boy's they liked and that they planned on going to a party. Katie inquired about what else the girls said. Danie said they stopped talking about it when she was spotted around the corner. They prayed together and headed for bed.

It was another sleepless night for Katie. She not only thought about Franklin, but also wondered what party the girl's would be talking about. She knew in her heart that if they stopped talking when Danie arrived it was not good news. She needed to talk to Valerie about it. She knew they were having some problems with the girls, usually after a visit with their father. She thought back to when she was fourteen. She was sixteen when her parents died and pregnant at seventeen. She shuddered as she thought about the trials of raising teenagers in this messed up world. Finally, she fell asleep with Tiger lying at the foot of her bed.

After Sunday school, she thought she would try to catch Valerie and talk to her, but did not get a chance to. She was having dinner at Tim's parents and needed to leave. She decided to call her later that night. When she did call, she told her about the conversation she had with Danie. Valerie said they were spending the next weekend at their father's house and she would talk to him about it. He was more lenient with the girls than she was. They could not go anywhere without her knowing and she would check up on them. Their father would let them go anywhere they wanted and never checked to make sure that was where they were. Valerie remembered what she was like at that age and tried to be vigilant.

Katie stood in the kitchen having coffee and thought again about Franklin. She promised Tim that she would watch for any signs of trouble. She did not want Tim to follow her and continue to drive her around. She yelled for the kid's to get ready, and she picked up the list of items she needed to get to complete her shopping for Thanksgiving dinner. Only four more days to make sure she had everything she needed. The next three nights she would be making candies and cookies. She thought about how her mother and grandmother would start baking days before and silently hoped she would be able to put together a feast that would make them proud.

Work went well and was busy which kept her mind occupied. The kid's would be home around 3:30 and promised to call her when they got home. She sent a text to Tim letting him know she was going to the store then home. Stacy waited for her so she could walk her to her car. The parking lot was empty, except for a few of the employee's vehicles. When she reached her car, she remembered her dream and looked in the back seat. She even opened the trunk to look inside then laughed at herself for thinking he would be hiding in her trunk.

The rest of the week went by without any sign of Franklin. Katie felt confident that he would not show up again. She allowed herself to relax and concentrate solely on Thanksgiving. She wanted to begin a new tradition and began jotting down different ideas. Finally, she decided that since it was Thanksgiving, they should begin what she would call a Thanksgiving testimony. This would be the first year. She went out to the yard, played with Tiger, and searched for the perfect tree branch. She then went to the shed and rummaged around until she found what she was looking for. She found an old window frame in the barn and cleaned it up. She thought about painting it, but really liked the rustic appearance. She laid her treasures on the table and began thinking about the next steps. Robert and Danie were curious and asked several questions that she responded with a simple, "Wait and see."

Wednesday night she stayed home from church so she could begin some of the preparations for Thursday. She needed to finish her Thanksgiving testimony project, make the salads and pies, then pull out her best China and tablecloth.

*Katie's Story*

She stayed up late working on her project. The window frame had nine smaller frames. Taking the tree branch that she coated with polyurethane, she arranged it in the middle of the frame using glue and heavy staples to secure it in place. In the smaller frames, she inserted pictures of the family, using cardboard and hooks to hold them in place. The branches had little hooks attached. She then had small pieces of card stock and sat them next to the finished project. She would have each person write down something he or she was thankful for and hang it on the hook. She would have Tim and Todd hang it for her. She thought about all the things she was thankful for and wondered if she would have enough hooks on her tree branch.

The next morning she busied herself in the kitchen. She had a lot of cooking to do and was slightly frustrated at her lack of skills in the kitchen. She enlisted Robert and Danie giving them task like peeling potatoes and cutting vegetables for the stuffing. She stopped periodically to look at the mess she was making and look at the clock to see how much time she had to get things done. Valerie called a couple of times to check on her and each time Katie told her things were fine, not to show up until five. At four-thirty, she looked around her house and breathed deeply. "Ready," she said relieved. The table was set, the meal was the same as finished and she was even dressed in her favorite dress.

Everyone was amazed and impressed with her accomplishments. Todd teased her about her Thanksgiving testimony tree but then added that it was a great idea. Tim was equally as impressed and told everyone he had read somewhere that if a man found a woman who could cook and carried a Bible, he needed to marry her. Before the meal, each person filled out their card and placed it on the tree. Later, they would tell each other what they had written down and why.

Todd read from the Bible, which he did every thanksgiving. [15]"Psalm 107:1, Give thanks to the Lord, for he is good; his love endures forever." He looked around at everyone and asked them to bow their heads in prayer. Katie looked around at the family as they gathered around the table and thanked God for giving her a loving family.

# Chapter Five

It had been nearly a week and Katie still had not heard from or seen Franklin. Daily, she thought less about him and assumed he had gone back home. She still made sure that when she parked her car it was in clear view and close to the door. She looked around her surroundings and made mental notes of everything and everyone around her. Although she was thankful that her brother installed the security camera system, she believed now that it was a waste of time and money. Her brother and Tim did not share the same opinion.

Just as she was about to call it a night the phone rang. It was April. Katie could hardly hear her because of the music in the background. Katie quickly grabbed some paper and a pen and jotted down an address. She told Robert that she needed to leave for a while and to keep his phone on and near. Her mind was racing, she was not sure if she should pick April and Susan up and then go to Todd's or call Todd first. April said she needed a ride and admitted that she had been drinking. She thought back to the one time she drank and how Tim picked her up. She remembered clearly the look of hurt on his face. She slowed down and located the right house by the sound of the loud music and the people milling around outside.

Pulling along the side of the road, she began to feel angry with the girls for their lack of respect for their mom and for Todd. She wondered whose house she was at and if there were any adults around. She was determined to find out what was going on before she left. Thinking she should investigate she walked along the side of the house to the back. She smelled a strange sweet smoky odor that she assumed must be what pot smelled like. As she approached the back of the house, she could see through the open window. She looked inside and could see at least a dozen teenagers' standing around and laughing. She made her way to the back door and found it was open. She did not think about ringing the bell or knocking, instead she walked right in and started looking for anyone who appeared to be an adult. After several minutes of walking through rooms filled with drinking and drunk teenagers, she did not find anyone who was of age. She turned and walked back outside and called Todd then she called the police department. As she hung up, she spotted April and called her over.

"Where is Susan?" she asked angrily.

"She left with Willey," she said, "about ten minutes ago."

Fear gripped Katie, "She left, who is Willey, was he drinking?" she demanded.

"Her boyfriend, and yes he drank, but he isn't drunk!" she snapped back sarcastically.

"Oh dear God," she said and began praying for Susan's safety. "Get in the car, Todd is on his way." She took April's arm and directed her to the car. "Where were they going?"

"To the store, they ran out of chips." April told her. "Why did you call Todd?" she said and began to cry.

"Because he is responsible for you, now what store?" her voice showed she was irritated and frightened.

"I don't know," she said as she lay down in the back seat. "I don't feel good." was all she got out of her mouth before she got sick.

Katie could see the police car coming around the corner and turned to see another one coming from the other direction. She instructed April to stay put and she went to meet the officer who pulled in the front of the driveway. She explained that she walked through the house and did not see any adults. Within a couple more minutes, there were another three patrol cars and Todd was behind them.

Valerie ran to the car and looked inside; she turned sharply toward Katie her eyes wide and questioning.

"Susan apparently left ten minutes before I got here with her boyfriend Willey," she said, "April said to the store, but didn't know which one."

"Boyfriend, store, what?" she almost screamed. "You two have a lot of explaining to do!" Turning back to Katie, "Their father is on his way too, I hope he is happy."

Todd spoke to an officer and learned that the owner of the house was out of town for the weekend. Their son, who is twenty-one years old decided to have a party for his brother without his parent's knowledge. The brother was seventeen and invited several of his friends. Most of the teenagers were between the ages of fourteen and seventeen. Within minutes, other vehicles with concerned parents started parking along the street and searching for their children.

Most of the activity had died down and there still was no sign of Susan. Valerie was a basket case and April was passed out in the backseat. Ken, Valerie's ex-husband, stood talking with Todd. When the two headed toward Valerie, she grew furious and began demanding to know why he did not keep them from going to the party.

"I talked to them about what you told me and they said they were just pulling a prank on Danie to see if she would tell on them." His response was curt. "Right now I think we need to concentrate on locating Susan and sort the rest out later." He turned and opened the car door and yelled at April to wake up. Once she woke up, she again started getting sick. Frustrated he turned to the others, "A lot of help she will be!" and slammed the door shut. "I will start driving around and see if I can spot anyone, can you handle that one?" he snapped at Valerie.

"Yes!" she matched his anger.

Katie volunteered to take April to her house and try to sober her up. Meanwhile Todd and Valerie would try to find out who Willey is and go to his house. Katie rolled all the windows down to allow the smell to escape, she also hoped the cold air would wake April up and perhaps help her sober. By the time they arrived at the house, Katie was able to get some additional information from her niece. She called Todd and told him Willey's last name and the street name he lived on. April did not know the house number; just that it was a yellow house with a large snowman in the front yard.

It took some doing, but she was able to get April in the shower and got her cleaned up. Now April sat at the table looking down at the cup of coffee in front of her. Katie told her she did not know if coffee really helped, but she heard it did and insisted she drink it. Katie also informed her that she would be cleaning her car out. At first, she wanted Robert and Danie to stay in their rooms, but then Katie decided they should actually see April and see what was going on. Perhaps, this could be a lesson for them she reasoned. She took the two outside to see the backseat of the car. She pointed out that this is what happens when someone drinks too much. She then directed

Katie's Story

them to sit in the living room or go back to bed. They wanted to stay up and make sure that everyone was going to be okay.

Valerie maintained contact with Katie and informed her each time that they still had not located Susan. They did find where Willey lived and his parent's stated that they had not seen him, but would call when he did arrive home. She had also called the hospital and no one fitting Susan's description was there. Katie continued to drill April about places that they may have gone. April could only think of the school grounds by the park on the Southside. Katie relayed that information and prayed that things would turn out.

"April, do you understand why we are all upset?" she asked.

"Yes." April answered.

"Right now we don't know where your sister is, if she is okay, hurt, or sick." She tried to explain. "Do you realize that people can get alcohol poisoning and die?" She uttered low trying to keep Danie and Robert from hearing her.

April looked at her for a long time then put her head down. "They could be at Willey's friend's house. He lives across the street from the high school," she admitted. "Willey drives a red truck; I think it's a ranger or something."

Katie quickly called and told Valerie what she learned. She then presented April with a bucket containing trash bags, paper towels, and wash clothes, pine cleaner, and pointed toward the car. April moved slowly with her head down then turned to Katie.

"I hope Susan is okay, we didn't mean..." she stopped and continued out to the car to begin cleaning her mess.

Katie had Robert and Danie go to bed, and then she paced from one end of the house to the other, periodically checking in on April. Once April finished cleaning up the mess, she thought they needed to have a frank talk. She thought about what to say as she paced and was horrified that she really did not know what to say to her. She never did anything like this at her age. Her parents, though not overly strict, were strict enough that it never crossed her mind to do something so stupid. The only thing she could really think to do was pray and ask God to direct her words.

Before Katie could start the conversation, April started talking to her. She told her how she did not really care for Willey, but Susan thought he was really something. She told her she called to have Katie pick her up because she did not want to go with her sister and did not want to stay at the party by herself. She admitted that going to the party was more Susan's idea and she went along because she did not want to look like she was scared. She wanted to fit in. She continued to tell Katie that at school, Susan was the popular one and she felt as if she were just the tag-a-long. She began to cry and asked if they could pray for her sister's safety. They did.

"You know, being a parent is not easy," Katie told April. "We don't have an instruction manual, other than the good word." She signed and again prayed that she would have the right words. "Your mom is scared; she is hurt, and she is angry." She took Aprils chin and lifted her face up so she could look directly in her eyes. "God knows we are human and are going to make mistakes. But, he also expects us to use our heads and understand the difference between right and wrong." April wiped away her tears and nodded her head in agreement. "You know when you are about to do something wrong, it is that small voice you hear in your heart and head, your conscious."

"I know, I wish I could be stronger and not give in." April cried softly.

"I know you do, and, you know, anytime you are not sure what to do, you can always talk to your parents, to Todd or even to me."

## Katie's Story

Tiger started barking alerting them that someone was coming up the driveway. Katie looked out the window and seen it was Todd and Valerie, and Ken was behind them. She watched to see if Susan was with them. Relief flooded over both Katie and April when Susan got out of the car.

Susan walked past Katie and sat down next to April. She was white and looked like she was about to burst into tears. She did not look up at anyone; she just sat with her hands in her lap. Todd, Valerie and Ken, talked quietly in the kitchen. When they finished talking, Ken said he was going home and would be at Todd's house the next day around noon. Todd and Valerie said they did not think they would go to church since it was already almost three in the morning. When everyone left, Katie prayed again for guidance for everyone and thanked God that Susan was found and safe. When she went to bed, she thanked God that she did not have these problems and prayed that God would continue to work in her children's lives.

# Chapter Six

It was almost eleven when Katie woke up and looked at the clock. She could hear the sound of the television and knew the kids were up. She walked in the kitchen and started the coffee pot. She wanted to talk to the kids about the commotion the night before, but also needed to talk to Valerie. She wanted to tell her about the conversation she had with April. She made the call and talked to Valerie for almost an hour. Valerie said that once they arrived home, the girls went to bed and they did not talk about anything. She said it was very quiet around the house, and that they were waiting on Ken to arrive.

Katie asked Robert and Danie to join her in the kitchen. She told them what happened and how serious the situation could have been. Danie was worried that the girls would be mad at her for telling on them. Robert said "Don't be undaunted by it." Katie laughed at his choice of words, he had been choosing a new word each day and found ways to use it. He had to tell Danie what is meant and then told her she did the right thing. Again, Katie thought about how amazed she was with Robert. Together they prayed for the family.

Tim called to see if everything was okay. He waited at church and when he did not see anyone, he was worried. She explained what was going on and apologized for not calling him. He asked if

## Katie's Story

they still wanted to go Christmas shopping. Katie had forgotten they made plans, but agreed it would be a good way to get their minds on something else. She needed to pick up a Christmas tree and some decorations and look at some things for the kids and other family members. They arranged to get together at one o'clock.

When they arrived, she parked next to Tim's truck. Jacob and Robert wanted to shop on their own and Danie ran into a few friends and wanted to shop with them. Tim and Katie looked at several artificial trees before finally selecting one that looked remarkably real. Although Katie would prefer a real tree, her allergies dictated what she could and could not have. They decided to finish their shopping then purchase the tree before leaving. Tim did not want to carry a tree through the mall. The next stop was a shop that sold handmade tree ornaments and decorations. Tim left Katie in the shop, telling her he needed to check on something and would be right back. After about thirty minutes, Katie made her selections on the decorations, purchased them, and waited on a bench in front of the shop for Tim to return.

When Tim returned, he had the whole crew with him. Katie thought how they all looked like they were up to something. She started to get up and Tim told her to stay put.

"I know we talked about waiting to get married, and we should, but," he got down on one knee and held out a small red box. He opened the box to reveal the most beautiful engagement ring Katie had ever seen. "Would you marry me, Katie?"

Before Katie could respond, she looked at the trio standing behind Tim. They were smiling and nodding their heads in approval and anticipation. She giggled and said yes. Tim placed the ring on her finger and to their surprise; they had an additional audience of other shoppers who started clapping and cheering them on. With the shopping completed and the official engagement, they went out for a celebration dinner. Afterwards, they would take their Christmas treasures home, set up the tree, and begin decorating.

As they pulled into the driveway, Danie was the first to notice Tiger was not barking. Katie instructed the kids to check and see if he had gotten loose while she started carrying things in the house. Jacob joined Robert and Danie and Tim assisted with getting the bags out of the car.

"Mom, he's gone!" Danie cried as she ran to the house. "His pen door is open and he is not here!"

"He couldn't have gone far." Katie told her. "Was the gate securely latched when we left?"

Robert and Jacob entered the house, "Yes mom, it was latched, I latched it myself."

Tim told Katie and Danie to stay put in the house and he and the boys would go look for him. Danie was distraught and insisted that someone had taken her dog. Katie tried to reassure her, but her efforts failed. When they heard footsteps on the porch they both ran to meet them, praying for good news. Unfortunately, they could not find him. They walked around the yard and toward the wooded area calling for him; they even drove around the area to see if he was running around. Tim took Katie to the side and told her they should look at the security footage.

Panic set in as they watched the footage. Someone walked from the road down the driveway and carried a long stick. They could not tell who it was because he or she was dressed in black and had a black facemask on. As they watched, the individual went around the house approaching each camera. The footage showed that the wood was actually a broomstick. Each camera went black as the intruder approached them. Danie was crying almost uncontrollably now. Tim told Jacob to call the police and Robert to call Todd. Katie tried to calm Danie down unsuccessfully.

When the police arrived, Tim showed them the footage and they walked around the house to look at each camera. They discovered that the camera's had been covered with what looked like black paint. They guessed that the stick was to knock the camera down or move it enough so that the person could place the paint over the lens without the face appearing. Tim told them about Franklin as they headed to the pen to investigate. With some relief, there was no sign of blood. One officer said they would check to see where Franklin was during the time they had left the house and returned. He also said that without proof, they would not be able to make an arrest. The officer added that the person in the video's face was never visible and because the person walked up the driveway, there was not a vehicle to try to identify.

Katie now joined Danie in borderline hysterics. Robert, Jacob and Ronnie found pictures of Tiger and said they would make lost poster's. April and Susan tried to comfort the hysterical Danie.

"It was Franklin!" Katie cried, "What if he hurt Tiger? What if he comes after Danie or Robert, or me?"

"I think it was him too," Todd said.

The next few days they contacted veterinary offices, animal shelters, and posted the lost posters. The contact number listed was Tim's instead of Katie's; they figured it would be safer not to list her number. Katie was fuming that they had to live in fear and constantly look over their shoulders. In an irate outburst one afternoon, she insisted that the cameras should have been set up higher so that no one could have seen them. Later she felt terrible for her temper tantrum and apologized. Just a few days before Christmas, they received their first break.

Tim received a call from a farmer who lives on Libertyville Road. Libertyville Road is between Ottumwa and Fairfield. The farmer thought he had Tiger and arranged a time for Tim to bring Katie to the farm. When they arrived, it was Tiger. He told them that he was tending to his cows when he heard a high-pitched squealing sound. He described it as the sound of a bad belt. He started toward the sound and seen a truck pulled over on the side of the road. As he approached, the truck pulled away. That was when he seen Tiger walking along the side of the road. Living in the country, he was accustomed to people dropping off their unwanted pets so he just called him over and took him in. He explained that he did not go to town much, which was why he did not know anyone was looking for the dog until today when he was in town. He said it was dark, but he was sure it was a silver Silverado, probably in the late nineties.

Tim called the officer assigned to their case and gave him the information. Danie declared this was the best pre-Christmas gift she could ever have.

Christmas was a wonderful celebration, although still under a cloud of fear, they rejoiced about the birth of Christ.

On New Year's Eve, they reflected on the past year and thanked God for the blessings he has given them. Valerie was doing well with her pregnancy; and Susan was expecting a baby too. Todd's little family was experiencing difficulties as well as wondrous moments, but they continued to Praise God in all things.

Tim and Katie set a wedding date for July 4. They wanted an outdoor wedding at their home. Nothing overly extravagant, but they wanted a cookout and fireworks. They too thanked and praised God during their struggles. Robert, Danie and Jacob were already making plans for rearranging the house once they all lived together. Overall, the year brought their families closer to each other and closer to God.

# Chapter Seven

The promise of a new fresh year was blurred with additional struggles for Katie. She was about to get in her car after leaving work when Franklin appeared. This time she was not fearful, but instead she was enraged. Without hesitation, she threw her belongings in the car and then stormed toward Franklin. Her hands formed fist and she felt as if she could tear him to pieces.

Stunned at her response, he backed up a couple of feet. "I don't want trouble. Katie, I just want to talk about us," he claimed.

"NO! THERE IS NO TALKING ABOUT US!" She yelled. "You have done enough! You have no business around me or my family."

"I wanted to apologize for how I behaved when we were married." He tried to continue, but Katie would not allow it.

"Leave, don't ever come back! We are DONE, D.O.N.E. done!" She turned to leave then turned back around. "I will call the police; I will see you in jail." Just as she finished her sentence, a police car pulled up and two officers stood next to Franklin.

To Katie's surprise, she watched as they read him his rights then placed handcuffs on him. Once he was securely in the back of the car, they told her they made a positive identification on the truck used to dump Tiger off. It belonged to Leo, who then admitted that he loaned it to Franklin. He also admitted that he knew what Franklin's plans were. Leo told the police that Franklin told him what he did and bragged about it. They also received a call from a female who told them Franklin was planning on showing up at the clinic today. The female caller, who did not identify herself, said she was worried that he would do harm to Katie. While Katie spoke with the officers, Tim called her. He checked his messages during his break at work and had a message from an unidentified female. She told him that Franklin planned to meet Katie when she left work. Katie told him what was happening and that she thought the caller may have been Rhonda.

Later that night Tim called her with more disturbing news. Judy, his ex-wife, showed up at his house while he was at work. Jacob was home when she arrived.

"Why now?" Katie asked uneasily.

"She told Jacob she just wanted to see how he was doing." Tim replied. He went on to tell her that Jacob did not know who she was since he had never met her. She left when he was young and she did not have family around. No one ever tried to keep in contact with them. Jacob said she asked many questions about Tim and his fiancé. She said she was doing better and wanted to be a part of their lives again.

"What does she mean of part of your lives?" her voice shaky.

"I don't know. All I know is Jacob is curious about her. He is confused, and I am not sure what to do or think." There was a brief pause before he continued. "She said she would stop by tomorrow to talk to me."

"Tomorrow?" Katie questioned.

"I know we had plans, but I think I should talk to her and find out what is going on." He sounded strange, "I think for Jacob's sake,

I should at least talk to her. I'm sorry Katie, don't worry, she doesn't mean anything to me any longer."

Katie did not feel reassured by his statement. She did not let on that she was worried, but she was. All she could think about that night and the next day was Judy. She wondered if she wanted to reconcile with Tim. In addition, she wondered if Tim would consider it because of Jacob. She worried about Jacob; she worried how Judy's return would affect him after all these years of not knowing his mother. She decided to talk to Heather about her fears. She still periodically attended the single mothers group so she decided she would attend this week and talk to Heather. She also thought it would be best not to say anything to Robert or Danie about Judy's return. She did not want them to fret, as she was fretting.

Heather was very sympathetic with Katie's fears. She told her that she did not think that Judy's return would have any influence on how Tim felt for her and the kids.

"Maybe this is what they both need to be able to move on with their life with you, closure." Heather told her. "I know from time to time Jacob has asked about his mother. He has wondered where she was, why she left, and why she never bothered to contact him. It is hard for a child to grow up not knowing anything about his or her parent's."

"I don't know Heather, it just seems like every time I turn around there is something going wrong." Katie said. "First Franklin and now Judy."

"You have to remember that Tim has stood by your side during this whole thing with Franklin. I believe he will continue by your side." She told her and then they prayed.

For the next few days, she talked to Tim, but did not see him. She tried to convince herself that it was because he was working late, but her mind tried to tell her it was because of Judy. She hoped to keep Judy's return a secret from Robert and Danie, but Jacob told Robert about it at school. Robert told Katie that Jacob said he really liked his mom. She was different from what he thought she would be. Danie was the one that asked if her return meant that they would not get married. Katie told her they still planned to get married, that nothing had changed, but she had doubts.

Jacob and Robert were busy on a project for the church youth group and Danie was working on a school report. Katie noticed during dinner that Jacob seemed quieter than normal. He was usually more talkative, but tonight he hardly said a dozen words. Tim finished loading the dishwasher while Katie put the leftovers in the refrigerator. Tim also seemed quieter than usual. When she asked him about work, he did not go into his usual animated details. Tim's ability to tell a good story was one of the things that attracted her to him. Whenever he told a story, his animation made the conversation more amusing. Again, trepidation gripped at her.

Tim was watching Katie as she cleared the table. He sensed she was not happy about something and wondered what he had done. He had been busy at work and was not able to spend as much time with her and the kids as he usually did. He wondered if his absence was bothering her a lot.

"Are you okay honey?" he asked her.

"Yea, fine," she quickly replied and walked into the living room. "How about you?' She said as she returned with a couple of cups retrieved from the coffee table.

"Fine, I am just tired." He took the cups and placed them in the dishwasher. "Work has been really busy this week, I am just about beat."

Katie sat down at the table. She wanted to ask him what was going on with him and Judy. She was sure he was spending extra time with her. She wondered if he was going to call off the wedding and get back together with his ex. Her heart started racing as she thought about it. She told herself to wait; she did not want to say anything in front of the kids. Danie came in and asked her mom if they were going to watch a movie. Katie was so absorbed in her thoughts that she did not hear her. After the third time of Danie saying "mom," she looked up absently.

"What, Danie I'm sorry, what did you say?"

"Are we going to watch a movie tonight?" Danie repeated, looking at her mom strangely.

"Oh, yea, pick one out and I will pop some popcorn." She started to move toward the kitchen when Tim told her that he and Jacob needed to head home. Startled, Katie turned to look at him. They always watched a movie and had popcorn when they came over for dinner. "Oh, okay," she said.

Tim had Jacob get his coat and he walked over to Katie to kiss her goodnight. He told her he loved her and she returned the sentiment half heartily. She popped the popcorn and sat through the movie without knowing what was on. Her mind was on Tim and their future.

When Robert and Danie went to bed, Katie pulled out her Bible and began to read. Her mind was troubled and she did not know what to do. After a few minutes, she gave up trying to read and went to bed. It was another sleepless night. During the night, she made up her mind that she had to confront him. She would not allow herself to sit around pining and worrying about this any longer. If he and Judy wanted to try to work things out, then they needed to end their relationship. Tomorrow after church, they would sit down and talk alone about the future.

When church services ended, she asked Tim if the two of them could talk. She wanted to talk without the kids being around. He looked at her confused, but agreed. They sent the kids to the matinee and the two of them went to his house. She pulled in the driveway behind him and almost burst out crying. He was standing at her door waiting for her to unlock it and get out. He wondered what was wrong with her.

Katie sat at the table and waited for Tim to make some coffee. She was not sure how to start the conversation. She really loved him but could not play second fiddle to his ex-wife. Her heart was racing, her palms were sweating and she could feel the beginning of a headache.

"What is wrong Katie?" Tim asked her as he placed their coffee on the table. "You have acted odd for a few days, did I do something wrong?"

She cleared her throat. "I was wondering the same thing about you. You and Jacob both have been acting strangely and you have not been coming over for dinner and…."

Tim interrupted her, "I have not been coming over for dinner because I have been working late" He tried hard not to sound upset, but he was. "You knew I have been working overtime on a project at work, I told you that."

Katie did not respond right away, she thought about what he said. He had in fact told her he was working late on some project. She wondered if she misread what was going on. Then she thought about his and Jacobs silence during dinner. "You and Jacob have seemed preoccupied, and I need to know if this has anything to do with Judy."

Tim could not believe his ears. This was the first disagreement he and Katie had since they started dating. "Well yes it does…."

Before he could finish Katie stood up and started putting her coat on. Crying she turned around and looked at him. "Then, I guess you and Judy can start over." She started toward the door, but he reached out and took her hand before she could get to far away.

"Start over, What?" He pulled her to him and looked in her eyes. "Judy and I are not starting anything. She has been part of the problem, but not like you think." He motioned for her to have a seat. "Sit down and let me explain."

He told her that Jacob was having a hard time since his mother's return. Judy told them she had cleaned up her act and wanted to get to know her son. As it turned out, she lied to Jacob. Judy really needed money and started to ask Jacob for a couple of bucks here and there. Then finally, one day asked him for three hundred dollars. He asked her why and she said she needed to pay a bill. When he told her he did not have that much money she got mad and stormed out of the house. When she returned, she begged him to ask Tim for the money.

"Oh Tim, I am sorry." Katie said.

"When Jacob told me what was going on I confronted Judy, she was shaking and sweating. I continued to press her for answers and she admitted she needed a fix."

"Does Jacob know?"

"I ordered her to leave or I would call the police and have her taken in. And yes, I told Jacob what was going on." Tim stood and shrugged his shoulders. "I hoped for Jacob's sake that she had changed, but she did not."

Katie thought for a moment about her accusations. "So, Jacob's silence has been because he is upset about his mother."

"Yes, and as for me, if you can imagine how I have tried to handle this." He took her hands in his. "Never once did it cross my mind to leave you for Judy. I have tried to help Jacob through this mess while working overtime." He smile, "And, why would I give you two dozen roses for Valentine's Day if I was planning on leaving you?"

"I know, I'm sorry, Tim I don't know what to say. Why didn't you tell me, I would have helped?" Katie questioned.

"Well, you were dealing with Franklin. I did not want you under any more stress. I should have told you, we are about to be husband and wife, I should not have kept anything from you."

"You were there for me the whole time. Through your own problems you still stood by me and helped me." She began crying again and wrapped her arms around his neck. "I'm so sorry."

"The overtime was volunteered; I wanted to save some extra money just in case after we got married you would need to quit work for a while." He told her then laughed. "Oh, Katie, you were jealous."

Katie began to laugh with him, but she still felt very embarrassed and foolish. She asked him why she would need to take any time off work. He said in case they decided to have a baby. She did not want to talk anymore about it so she quickly changed to subject. She told him the movies would be getting out soon and they needed to get the kid's picked up.

They drove separately so that she could go to the store and go home. She was glad she changed the subject. "Baby" she said as she drove. She did not know if she wanted to have another child. She would really need to pray about this.

# Chapter Eight

Katie planned to attend the single mother's support group and thought it would be a good idea for Susan to go with her. She thought Susan could use some advice from some of the women in the group. Valerie and Katie both tried to talk to her about her feelings, but she was shutting them out. Valerie agreed that it would be good for her to go.

When Susan told Willey she was pregnant, he broke up with her telling her he did not want children. He also insisted it was not his. He started making fun of her and telling all his friends that she was pregnant when he started dating her. Susan spent many days in her room; she was heartbroken and wanted to be alone. She thought between the morning sickness and her broken heart, that she would surly die.

"Susan, I know how hard this is going to be for you." Katie wanted so badly for her to open up to her. "You know you are never so far away from God that you can't take just one step and get back with him, don't you?"

Susan just looked out the window and did not respond. She thought about how the girls at school looked at her. They pointed fingers at her and laughed. When she would see Willey, he took off in the opposite direction. She was also sure that April now looked down on her when before she looked up to her. She could feel tears welling up in her eyes. She remained silent and was relieved when Katie did not try to persuade her into having another meaningful conversation.

Heather was pleased to see them arrive and welcomed them warmly. She told them they would be discussing Godly men. The women gathered around the tables, Susan sat on the opposite side of the room as Katie. After Heather opened in prayer, she began the session.

"As I mentioned before, tonight I want us to talk about and think about Godly men. Some of you have been married and some of you have not. A lot of you have dated someone then ended up breaking up because the relationship was not what you or what he thought it would be." She looked around the room as the women were nodding their heads and making comments about the men they dated or had even married. She allowed them to chat for a few minutes.

"Okay, last week I was visiting the school in which my daughter is a physical education teacher. She asked me to talk to them about men and abstinence. I asked the group of teenage girls what they looked for in a boyfriend." She stopped and shook her head. "You would be amazed at some of the responses I received. But, before I tell you what the responses were, I want to know what you look for in a boyfriend or future husband."

There were several answers. Some said he needed to work, others that he treated her kindly and loved her and her children. Katie could see that Susan was listening even though she pretended not to be. She figured Susan would think that her invitation to tonight's session was a set up, but Katie did not know what they would be discussing tonight.

"Katie, how about you. What do you look for in a future husband?" Heather asked.

Katie thought about it for a moment before she answered. "I guess, with Tim, I looked for a Christian, that he would be able to love my children and be a good man." She paused, "With Franklin, I think I just settled because I was lonely."

"Okay, let's start with [16]Ephesians 5:25, Look it up in your Bible please." She waited until they all found the verse then asked Susan if she would like to read it.

Susan rolled her eyes but opened her Bible and found the scripture. "Husbands, love your wives, as Christ loved the Church and gave Himself up for her.," she read in a monotone voice.

"Can anyone tell me what you think this means?" Heather asked.

There were a few different answers. Again, Susan pretended not to be paying any attention to anyone. One of the woman said she thought it meant that when you are married you would have problems, just as you do as a Christian, but that if you loved your wife as Christ loves, the bad times can be better. This started quiet a discussion among the women.

"Guess that means there are not any good men out there!" Susan said sarcastically.

The women did not know if they should laugh or be quiet. Some of them giggled and said they were few and hard to find. Susan smiled as some of the women made comments about the difficulty in finding a good man.

"Susan, can you elaborate on that?" Heather asked.

"You all know I am pregnant. My ex-boyfriend left as soon as I told him I was going to have his child. Men are mean," she said.

Heather could sense Susan's pain. "Let's look at another scripture. Go to [17]Colossians 3:19." She opened her Bible and read the scripture. "Husbands, love your wives and do not be harsh or bitter or resentful toward them." She closed her Bible and looked around the room.

"If the person you are dating is harsh, bitter or resentful to you, is he a Godly man? And, is he the best person for you to be dating or planning to marry?"

Individually, the women discussed parts of their personal experiences. Heather listened to each one give her account of their past relationships. After a few minutes, she pulled everyone's attention back.

"So, listening to you, I have discovered something that perhaps you have not. The next question I want you to think about, you do not have to answer me, just think about it. Have all the men you dated or married had the same traits?" She waited for a few minutes. "I know, from my own personal experience, that each man I dated and married, have been basically the same as the one before. I found that I was attracted to men who were somehow abusive to me."

"Why?" Susan asked her.

"I guess for me I was attracted to men who reminded me of my father. He was verbally abusive to mom and to us kid's."

"So why, I mean, if your dad was mean, why find a mean boyfriend?" Susan asked with real interest.

"Because it was familiar. I knew how to be the victim and not the victor." She looked at Susan, "Sometimes, we select the wrong man, just because he was nice to us or our hormones are really messed up."

Again, the ladies discussed amongst themselves for a little while. Since it was getting late, Heather let them talk without going into the next scriptures she selected. When it was time to close the session, she asked them to read [18]I Corinthians 7:1-40 and be prepared to talk next week about what they read.

On the way home, Katie thought about the group discussions. She hoped that the information would help Susan in the future. She also decided she should begin putting together pieces of information to share with Danie. Danie had never mentioned a particular boy, but she wanted to be ready to have a conversation about men. She was thankful that Tim and Todd talked to Robert for her. She dropped Susan off and headed home.

That night, she lay in bed and thought again about her own problem. Having a baby was a big step. She wondered if having a baby would be too much of a strain on their relationship, on their children or even their income. They were both making good money, but the kids will soon be old enough to begin looking at colleges. She already knew Robert wanted to attend a Christian college. She remembered when Danie was little. Tim did not have any problems changing her diaper or feeding her. "He is really a wonderful father," she said to the ceiling. "Oh, Lord, help me to be able to do whatever your will is. If Tim and I should be open to, or even decide to have children, we will raise our child to know and to love you."

# Chapter Nine

Valerie and Todd invited the family over for a spring welcoming party. Even though it was still chilly outside, they decided Todd and Tim could wear coats and barbeque. Danie was eager to see April and Susan and was excited to see the picture of the ultrasound. Valerie waited for everyone to be present before announcing if she was having a boy or girl. Todd did not even know the sex yet.

"Mom, when will Susan know what she is having?" Danie asked.

"Probably next month." She said as she thought again about how hard it was going to be for her. Todd, Valerie and Ken talked to Susan about what she wanted to do. It was a given that abortion was out, but there were other choices. She could keep the baby and the grandparent's would help her or she could put the baby up for adoption. Valerie was praying that Susan would keep the baby. Although she knew how hard it would be having two babies in the same house, she also knew she did not want to give up her grandchild. Ken was the one who said that if she decided on adoption, one of the parent's should step in and take over. He told them she was not old enough to make such a decision. Valerie told Katie that she and Todd had already planned to keep the baby, but they also wanted to give Susan the opportunity to think about what she should do.

*Katie's Story*

Everyone was gathering in the living room and begging to know what they were having. Todd was also ready to know. Valerie told everyone that they both agreed on what to name the baby. If it is a girl she would be Aquila Marie and if a boy Jeremiah Lee. Susan watched and listened from the kitchen doorway.

"Todd, we are having a little...." she looked around one last time teasing them, "Jeremiah Lee!"

Everyone started rejoicing and laughing and trying to see the ultrasound. Katie could see Susan straining to see without leaving her spot. Once Katie had the ultrasound in her hand, she took it to Susan.

"Susan, look at this little life, your little brother." She said as she handed the photo to her.

Susan slowly took the picture and pretended she did not care. When she looked at the photo tears began to flow down her face. She took her finger and outlined the little body. "Wow." She said and looked past Katie to her mom. "This is really a real live little person."

Valerie walked over to Susan and they hugged and cried. Susan finally let go of her mom. "I want to keep my baby, I know it will be hard, but I want her."

"Her?" Valerie said laughing.

Susan looked at her mom and straightened her shoulders, "Her, yep, she will be a she!" At that, she asked Danie and April to join her in the bedroom.

Susan closed the door and sat on the foot of the bed. She looked at April, "I am sorry that I made you feel like a tag-a-long. I really did not mean to hurt you. I love you, you're my sister." They hugged and cried. Looking at Danie, "And Danie, I am sorry I was mad at you for telling on us. You did do the right thing."

"So, you are going to keep the baby?" Danie smiled.

"Yes and the two of you are going to have to help me some!" She laughed then became serious. "I went to the group with Katie last week. I didn't want to, but mom said I had to go. They were talking about Godly men." She took a deep breath. "Willey was far from Godly! I know it's a little late, but I want to make a pledge right now, to not have sex until I am married."

In unison Danie and April said "Me too." They all decided to make it official by praying together and asking God to remind them of their agreement if he needed to.

"So, what about this Godly man thing?" April asked Susan.

"Well, I think it means that whoever we decide to date we should make sure he is a Christian. That he is nice to us and to our family." She stopped to think a minute then continued. "Like Todd and Tim."

The girls began talking about girl names for the baby. There was no mention of a boy's name. They all agreed that Susan was having a little girl. They reasoned that they would need one more girl to even the number of boys and girls. They looked up several names on the computer and discussed which would be the best one. They all agreed on Hannah Adriel. Hannah means gracious and Adriel means the flock of God. They all rushed out to let everyone know what they decided.

When it was time for her ultrasound, she insisted that April and Danie be there. Now confirmed and the girls were right, she was having a little girl. The three girls were giddy and wanted to go shopping for girl clothes right away. Valerie and Katie agreed that a shopping spree was what they all needed. Katie also wanted to get some more decorations for the wedding. A trip for Iowa City was planned for the following Saturday.

Katie was telling the girls in the office about the ultrasound and their shopping date. Iowa City was one of her favorite places to shop. She started telling them about the list of baby items the girls had prepared when one of the nurses told her she had a visitor. She walked out the door to see Rhonda waiting for her.

"Rhonda, are you okay, what happened?" she asked. Katie again thought how Rhonda didn't look well.

Rhonda asked if they could talk. Katie asked her if she could hang around the office for an hour then they could go somewhere. Rhonda said she could and would wait in the cafeteria. As Rhonda walked away Katie prayed for her. She knew in her heart that something was wrong.

The last hour of work Katie wondered what was wrong with Rhonda. She wondered what she wanted to talk about. "Maybe she is going to apologize" she said as she placed some files on the desk.

Stacy was walking in the door, "Who?" she questioned. She looked at Katie and realized that she was talking to herself and laughed.

Katie turned red, "Oh, woops, I was thinking about Rhonda."

"She is here" Stacy questioned.

"Yes, in the cafeteria waiting for me. She wanted to talk to me." Katie almost asked if Rhonda was sick, then changed her mind. "Well, I guess I will find out."

As they walked out the door they decided to go to the park. It was fairly close and they could find a bench or sit in a shelter. When Rhonda continued to follow Katie she realized she needed a ride.

"How did you get here?" Katie asked as she unlocked the car doors.

Rhonda told her that she had a doctor's appointment earlier and brought the bus. When Katie said she didn't see her in the lobby Rhonda told her she was there to see Doctor Henry. Katie was surprised and instantly felt dread wash over her. Doctor Henry is the cancer specialist at the clinic. Katie and Rhonda didn't talk anymore until they arrived at the park. They walked to an open shelter and Katie was glad that no one was around.

"Katie, I wanted to tell you again how sorry I am about Franklin. I feel like everything is my fault." Rhonda told her.

"No, Rhonda, it is not your fault. Really, Franklin made his own choices."

"I know, but I introduced you. Then I found out what happened in Nevada. Katie, I didn't know any of that until after I told him where you worked." Her voice was shaky and she had tears in her eyes.

"Rhonda, why did you really come here today?"

Rhonda looked toward the playground and watched a couple of kids playing on the merry-go-round. "I always thought I would like to have kids." She said absently. "Leo left me after...." She started crying, "I have cancer, stage four."

Katie gasped and reached for Rhonda hugging her and crying. "I am so sorry."

"I just wanted to tell you how sorry I am before..."

Katie understood that she needed closure and told her that she was forgiven. Rhonda explained that the cancer was very aggressive and they gave her about three months to live. She told her Leo said he was not going to watch anyone die and left. After he left she moved in with her mother. Rhonda told Katie that her mother was still bitter about her father's death. He passed away from cancer two years ago. Katie listened to Rhonda and prayed that God would open a door for her to be able to witness to her friend.

"Rhonda, would you mind if I prayed for you right now?" Katie asked. Rhonda told her that she could pray. While Katie prayed, Rhonda wondered if prayer really worked or if it was a waste of time. She hoped it would work.

They continued to talk for a while then Katie took her home. She told Rhonda that Valerie and Susan were expecting babies and that she and Tim were discussing children. She explained that during their pre-marriage counseling, which is a requirement of the church, they have discussed if they wanted or should have children.

# Chapter Ten

Valerie watched as Katie paced the floor in the hospital delivery room. She was on the phone with Todd while Katie was on the phone with Tim. April, Susan and Danie waited in the waiting room. Katie was the first to hang up her phone. She stood looking out the large window that overlooked the parking lot. From here, she would be able to see when Todd and Tim arrived. Valerie ended her call with Todd.

"Come sit down." She told her nervous sister-in-law.

"What did he say?" She asked as she sat down.

"He and Tim will be here soon, they have to load the fishing gear."

Todd and Tim decided it was a nice day to take the three boy's fishing. They went to a spot in Bloomfield, a neighboring town that is roughly thirty minutes away. While they were fishing, Katie, Valerie and the girls were putting the final touches on the wedding decorations. Unfortunately, Jeremiah had plans of his own.

The nurse popped her head in and asked if Susan could come in. Valerie told her yes and in came a very distressed daughter.

"Mom, you are three weeks early, will Jeremiah be ok? Will you be ok?" she asked.

"Yes, the doctor said everything would be fine." She motioned for Susan to come closer to the bed. "The guys will be here soon, I just hope soon enough for Todd to be here for the delivery!" she laughed.

"Mom, that's not funny!" Susan told her sharply.

"I know that we were not expecting this. Susan, it will be fine."

Katie remembered when she had Robert and Danie. Both times she was about two weeks early. She remembered the look on Danny's face when he first laid eyes on Robert. She smiled as she remembered how excited he was that it was a boy. She thought how sad it was that he never had the chance to hold Danie. She watched Valerie and thought about how well her pregnancy has gone. She hoped that when she and Tim decided to have children, her pregnancy would be as smooth as Valerie's. Her thoughts were interrupted when the doctor came in the door.

The doctor on duty happened to be Steward Ellis, a member of their church. "Susan, how are you doing young lady?" he asked as he walked toward Valerie. She responded that she was fine and that she was concerned for her mother. "No worries, God and I have this covered!" He winked at Valerie and turned toward Katie. "Where are the men folk?"

"On their way, they were fishing in Bloomfield." Katie told him.

"Valerie, do you mind if Susan and Katie are in here for this?

"Its fine, they can stay." She looked at Susan, "You should know what is coming."

After a few minutes Steward confirmed they would be having a son really soon. He asked again if Valerie wanted any medications and she insisted she would have the baby without meds. Satisfied he said he would see her soon. As he was walking out the door Todd was about to walk in.

"It's about time you got here son! Your misses will be having that little boy soon," he laughed.

"How soon doc?" Todd asked.

"Probably within a couple of hours, could be less, she is progressing right along." At that, he walked out the door.

Katie and Susan left Todd with Valerie and headed to the waiting room. Tim waited by the door watching for her. Katie laughed at the large smile on his face. She thought he looked like he was the expectant father. They sat down and chatted for a few minutes. Katie's phone beeped, it was Todd letting them know the baby was almost here. About five minutes later, he sent a picture of Jeremiah. Katie thought he looked a lot like Todd. The crew of teenagers began asking a hundred questions. They wanted to know the weight, how long he was, when they could see him and how was Valerie. Katie laughed as she told them all was well and Todd forgot to send the specifics. She told them they would see the baby in probably an hour or so. True to her word, in an hour they were able to see Jeremiah through the window.

Katie waited at Todd's for the family to come home. She spent part of the morning cleaning the house and the other part preparing lunch for everyone. She could not wait to hold her nephew. As she waited her phone rang, it was Rhonda.

"Hi Rhonda, what's up?" she asked as she placed the silverware on the table.

"Katie, can you come over? I really need to talk to you." Rhonda asked in an almost panicked voice.

"I can, but it will be a little bit." Katie told her about the baby and explained she would head over around two. After she hung up, she wondered what was wrong and prayed for wisdom and strength.

*Katie's Story*

The homecoming celebration ended with a tired little baby and mommy. Todd thanked Katie for her help as he walked her to her car. He also asked if she was sure, she wanted to go to Rhonda's alone. Katie ensured him that she no longer feared Rhonda's motives. She added that she felt that Rhonda wanted to make peace. "Perhaps she also wants to make peace spiritually." She said hopefully.

Rhonda was sitting in her room with the curtains closed and lights out. Her mother, Sharon, told Katie that she had been in her room for three days. She was a small fragile looking woman, and Katie guessed she was in her late seventies. She did not seem very friendly and it appeared to Katie that she did not want her there. She pointed toward Rhonda's door and turned to leave.

"Let me know if you need anything." She stated gruffly over her shoulder.

Rhonda was reclined in an old beat up recliner. A heavy fleece blanket lay across her sliming body. Her eyes sunk in and there were dark circles around them. She had a stocking cap on, but Katie could tell she no longer had any hair. As she approached her, she spotted a small Bible sitting on the table next to the chair. A glimmer of hope stirred in Katie's heart. She sat on the side of the bed facing her sick friend.

"Thanks for comin," Rhonda said weakly. "Think I'll get to the point in case I die first."

Startled Katie replied, "Ok."

"I went to church only when g-ma and pa took me. That was on Christmas and Easter." She looked at Katie as if she was trying to read her expression. Apparently satisfied that Katie did not respond negatively she continued. "Now, all I really know for sure is that Jesus was born on Christmas and he was crucified and came back from the dead on Easter." Again, she paused, "That about right?"

Katie prayed quickly before speaking. "Well, yes. Of course, some of the middle stuff is missing. Do you want to know what the missing parts are?" She questioned hoping she did. When Rhonda nodded her head, she continued.

"Well, let's start with the birth. I am not going to go into major detail; I just want to clear some things up." She said as she scooted back on the bed and crossed her legs. [19]"God sent us his son, Jesus, born of a virgin, Mary. He did this because he wanted to save us. You may have heard the scripture, [20]John 3:16, For God so loved the world, that he gave his only begotten Son, that whosoever believeth in him should not perish but have everlasting life."

Rhonda nodded her head that she had heard that. Katie explained briefly that Jesus was born and lived with his mother who was Mary, and with Joseph.

"Now, he was crucified. He was accused of [21]blasphemy and [22]crucified. However, he was sent to us to live among us and then to die for us. [23]His death on the cross was to take on the sin of the world, our sins." She stopped and thought for a moment. [24]"Each of us are sinners, we all sin in different ways. One sin in no worse than the other, it is still sin. Through Jesus' death we can receive grace and be forgiven of our sins." She took a deep breath and thought back to the rest of what Rhonda asked her. "He was crucified and [25]three days later he arose from the dead. [26]He now sits at his father's right hand."

"I thought he walked with us, g-ma always said he walked with us." Rhonda questioned with real interest.

"He does, [27]in our hearts. When we allow him into our heart that is where he is. He is with us every minute of every day."

Katie opened the Bible and started looking up scripture and explaining them to Rhonda. Almost two hours later Rhonda was overly exhausted and fell asleep in the chair. Katie covered her up, knelt down, and prayed next to her. When she was finished praying, she found some paper and pen and jotted a note for Rhonda. When she opened the door, Sharon was standing in the hall with her hands on her hips.

"I don't like you filling her head with that Jesus nonsense!" she snapped. "For God so loved the world, well, if he did, my husband would still be here." She pushed past Katie and opened the front door. "If she asks you to come back that is fine, but otherwise, well just leave."

As Katie drove home, her heart was breaking for her friend and her mother. She felt inadequate to try to lead them to God. How could she possibly change the way they feel in such a short amount of time. She needed to call her pastor and get some advice.

# Chapter Eleven

Today was the big day; she and Tim would become one. The forecast said it would be in the low eighties with no wind. Katie was in her room fixing her hair and getting her make-up on. She could hear Tim laughing in the back yard and smiled. She refused to look out the window; she did not want to see him until she walked down the aisle. She moved toward the window and listened with her eyes closed. She could smell the aroma of sweet smoky meat cooking mixed with roses. She smiled as she listened to the kids talking excitedly about the wedding.

She talked to Todd a few months ago and asked if it would be okay if Robert and Danie gave her away instead of him. He thought that was a great idea. She thought about her father and again wished he was the one giving her away. She opened a box on her dresser that Todd gave her that morning. The box contained two treasures for Katie. Sonny, their uncle, was not able to attend the wedding, but wanted Katie to have something that belonged to her parents. She pulled out a handkerchief that had her mother's name embroidered on it. Katie's grandmother made the handkerchief for her daughter on her wedding day. The next item she pulled out of the box was a set of cufflinks. Her father wore the cufflinks at their wedding. Katie held the treasures to her heart.

She looked at the clock and realized she needed to finish getting ready. She picked up her dress and thought about Rhonda. Katie asked Rhonda to assist with picking out the wedding attire. Since this was Katie's third wedding and Tim's second, they did not want to wear formal wedding attire. Katie would be wearing a lacy summer dress in white with a blue belt and red shoes. Danie, Valerie, Susan and April were wearing blue and red summer dresses with white flip-flops. Tim, Robert, Jacob, and Luke choose to wear white shorts with red tops and blue sandals. Todd was wearing white shorts and white top with red and blue sandals. Rhonda thought it was all very appropriate for a wedding on the Fourth of July.

She could hear the men talking about the diagram she and Tim prepared. Tim was busy directing the men as they were setting up the tables and chairs in the back yard. The chairs needed to be set up in the center of the yard facing the pond and leaving a walkway for the bride to walk down during the ceremony. Tables and chairs were set up on the far side of the yard, close to the fire pit. A hog had been cooking since early in the morning and filled the air with a wonderful aroma making everyone hungry.

Valerie and the girls were busy decorating the columns that outlined the walkway leading to the pond. The bride and groom would stand at the entrance of the columns. Instead of a unity candle, the new family unit would each light a tea candle. The candles would float on the pond on a small body board. The three girls came up with the idea to use glasses filled with red, white and blue sand and place flags in them for each table centerpiece. Everything was red, white and blue, even the wedding cake.

Some of the women from the single mother's support group helped Heather with the meal. They prepared potato and macaroni salad, Jell-O salads, chips, baked beans, vegetable and meat trays, and fresh fruit. "A real picnic meal," Heather told them. Rhonda mixed the punch and asked one of the women to carry it to the table.

Katie watched Rhonda as she helped the women in the kitchen. She had spent several days over the last two weeks talking with Rhonda. Her mother seemed to soften up a little with each visit. Katie asked Rhonda during their last visit if she wanted to ask Christ into her heart. Rhonda did not respond, instead she turned her head away and looked out the window with a troubled mind.

Katie worried about her friend. Each day she seemed to grow weaker. She sensed it would not be long and she would be gone. She thought about the conversation she had with Tim a week ago. They planned on going on a honeymoon to North Carolina the morning after the wedding. Katie asked Tim if they could postpone the honeymoon. She told him about her talks with Rhonda, and that her mother was now talking with them. She feared that Rhonda would not be around when they returned and she wanted to be there for her. Tim understood and agreed that Rhonda and her mother's salvation were more important than a honeymoon.

The wedding was a celebration of love for one another, for God and love for their country. The weather man was right and the temperature was perfect. A variety of fireworks were set off when it was dark, which made Tiger upset and he began howling loudly making everyone laugh. The church band played until after midnight. When the last guest left, Tim and Valerie sat next to the pond and talked about the wedding.

Tim took Katie's hand and pulled her up from the chair.

"Dance with me again." He said and pulled her close.

# Katie's Story

"I would love to my husband." She laughed.

The day after the wedding Katie called Rhonda to check on her. She called her the second day after the wedding and Sharon told her she was sleeping. Sharon told Katie that Rhonda was not doing well, so Katie and Tim went to see her. When they arrived, she looked like she was already gone. Katie could feel a lump in her throat. Sharon gently touched Rhonda's arm and told her she had company.

Rhonda looked up at Katie from the bed where she was laying. "I have a question." her voice was low and raspy. "I have not been a good person, will Jesus forgive me of all the wrongs I have done?" Her chin was quivering and Sharon was crying.

[28]"He will forgive all your sin's and throw them in the sea of forgetfulness and never think of them again." Katie told her. "All you have to do is ask him."

Sharon now looked at Katie with begging eyes. "Will he also forgive me?"

"Oh, yes!" Katie responded while wiping away her own tears. "Are you both ready?"

Rhonda and Sharon said they were ready and Katie asked them to repeat after her. "Dear Lord Jesus, I know I am a sinner and I ask you to please forgive me of my sins. I believe that you are the Son of God and that you died for my sins. I ask that you give me your grace. In Jesus name. Amen."

Sharon and Rhonda were hugging and crying, as were Katie and Tim. Sharon was about to go prepare some iced tea when Tim noticed Rhonda's breathing. He gently touched Sharon's arm and told her it was time. Sharon and Katie both knelt down next to Rhonda and Tim prayed silently. Sharon rubbed her daughters hand and told her how much she loved her and that she could go home now. Rhonda whispered thank you to Katie, looked at her mother, and told her she loved her and closed her eyes for the last time.

Katie and Tim sat on the deck of their cabin in Hot Springs, North Carolina. The cabin was in a secluded area of the woods. From their deck they could listen to the sounds of singing birds and rustling creek.

Katie smiled at Tim and held tight to his hand. "What a romantic getaway." She told him.

"I think we should stay another week, Mrs. Smyth." Tim replied and winked at his wife.

"Well, Mr. Smyth, we should" She looked at him and smiled. "I was just thinking. You and I have a renewed life." She squeezed his hand. "So does Rhonda and Sharon."

[29]"Therefore, if anyone is in Christ, he is a new creation. The old has passed away; behold, the new has come. 2 Corinthians 5:17." He said softly. "You are right, we are renewed.

# Preface

[1]  John 3:16, King James Version

**Part One Renewed Hope, Chapter Two**

[2]  Psalm 18:2, King James Version

**Part One Renewed Hope, Chapter Three**

[3]  Isaiah 41:10, The Message

**Part One Renewed Hope, Chapter Four**

[4]  Acts 13:22, King James Version

[5]  Psalm 10, The Message

[6]  Joshua 1:9, King James Version

**Part One Renewed Hope, Chapter Six**

[7]  Moore, Beth. Get Out Of That Pit: Straight Talk about God's Deliverance. Nashville: Integrity Publishers, 2007

**Part One Renewed Hope, Chapter Eleven**

[8]  Proverbs 22:6, King James Version

**Part One Renewed Hope, Chapter Twelve**

[9]  Gaither, William J, He Touched Me: 1963

[10]  John 4:28, King James Version

[11] Luke 15:11-32, King James Version
[12] Jeremiah 33:3, King James Version

**Part Two Renewed Life, Chapter One**
[13] I Samuel 1:9-17, The Message

**Part Two Renewed Life, Chapter Three**
[14] Psalm 121, New International Version

**Part Two Renewed Life, Chapter Four**
[15] Psalm 107:1, King James Version

**Part Two Renewed Life, Chapter Eight**
[16] Ephesians 5:25, English Standard Version
[17] Colossians 3:19, Amplified Bible
[18] I Corinthians 7:1-40, King James Version

**Part Two Renewed Life, Chapter Ten**
[19] Matthew 1:18, King James Version
[20] John 3:16, King James Version
[21] Mark 14:64, King James Version
[22] Mark 15:20-37, King James Version
[23] I Peter 2:24, King James Version
[24] I John 1:8, King James Version
[25] John 20:1, King James Version
[26] I Peter 3:22, King James Version
[27] Ephesians 3:17, New Living Translation

**Part Two Renewed Life, Chapter Eleven**
[28] Micah 7:18-19, King James Version
[29] 2 Corinthians 5:17, King James Version